The Courage to Cross Horizons

A story of survival, resilience, and triumph

ZINAH MINEYAHL

The Courage to Cross Horizons
A story of survival, resilience, and triumph
"From the rugged highlands of Ethiopia to the corporate boardrooms of
America, Zinah Mineyahl's story is one of survival, resilience, and
triumph. Escaping civil war with nothing but courage, he built a new life
in a new land, rising from $10 in his pocket and broken English to become
a leader in one of America's largest industries. More than a memoir, this is
a story of hope for anyone who has ever dreamed of crossing their own
horizons."

ABAY RIVER
MEDIA

The Courage to Cross Horizons
© 2025 Zinah Mineyahl
Contact: zinah@abayrivermedia.com
Website: www.abayrivermedia.com

This memoir reflects the author's personal experiences and memories. Some names and identifying details have been changed to respect privacy.

ISBN: 979-8-218-85113-2 (eBook)
ISBN: 979-8-218-85114-9 (paperback)
ISBN: 979-8-218-85115-6 (hardcover)
Printed in the United States of America

Dedications

For Enana,

Who walked with me through every challenge and every move,

Who turned every house we lived in into a home, even when we had to leave it all behind.

Who raised our children with grace and wisdom when my work kept me far away,

And who carried the weight of silence and solitude on nights I could not be there.

Who shoveled snow while I sat in warm offices,

Who decorated walls only to take them down for another journey,

Who never once cast doubt when I stumbled, even when I came home with a broken arm.

Your strength made my strength possible.

Your love is the quiet foundation beneath every chapter of this story.

Without you, there would be no story to tell.

To my family, past, present, and future whose love and sacrifices made this journey possible. To the mentors and friends who lifted me when I stumbled, and to the generations to come who will walk new paths with courage.

TABLE OF CONTENTS

Epigraph

"Courage is not the absence of fear, but the triumph over it. The brave man is not he who does not feel afraid, but he who conquers that fear."
Nelson Mandela

ACKNOWLEDGMENTS

No journey is taken alone. I owe deep gratitude to my wife, Enana, who stood by me through every move, every challenge, and every moment of uncertainty. To my children, Mahlet and Markos, whose smiles gave me reason to endure. To my siblings and extended family, who reminded me of my roots, and to my mentors such as Anthony Hayes , Jasper, and many others, who lifted me when I was learning to spread my wings.

To Adebabay Birru,

Whose persistent encouragement served as both catalyst and compass in the writing of this memoir.

Your unwavering insistence that my story be preserved, and your genuine enthusiasm for every fragment I shared, affirmed the importance of committing memory to record.

This work stands not only as a reflection of my own journey but also as a testament to the value of kinship in shaping history and legacy.

I thank my community, both Ethiopian and American, for the bonds of support, friendship, and love. And above all, I give thanks to God, whose hand carried me when I could not walk on my own.

Preface

I came to the United States in my early twenties with ten dollars in my pocket and broken English. My journey began as a fugitive running for my life and became a story of survival, resilience, and triumph.

This memoir is not simply the story of one man; it is a story of many. It is about those who flee oppression, who cross rivers and deserts in search of freedom. It is about immigrants who rebuild from nothing, who carry both the pain of exile and the hope of renewal. It is about family, faith, and the courage to rise after every fall. Many were not as lucky as I am and perished somewhere in a similar journey. I feel fortunate to share my story with you.

I wrote this book for my children, my grandchildren, and the generations that will follow so that they know where we came from, what we endured, and what is possible when determination meets opportunity.

May these pages serve not only as memory, but as encouragement to anyone who faces hardship: keep climbing, for there is always a horizon to cross.

Part I: Roots

Chapter 1 – My Roots

I was born in Ethiopia, in what was once called Gojjam Province. My parents met in their early twenties, both carrying dreams of their own. At the time, marriages were arranged by parents who decided who their children would marry and when. My mother rejected this tradition. She left her village, crossing the Abay River and leaving behind her toddler son, my older brother, to seek a new life. She came to the town of Mota, where she met my father, who had also refused the marriage arranged for him by his family.

Together, they made their own choice to move to Debre Markos and start a family on their own terms. I was born of that decision, to parents who chose their own path in a nation where millions still followed the lives laid out for them.

The thread of courage runs deep in my family, stitched across generations of struggle and survival.

The story of who I am begins long before I was born. It is written in courage, resilience, and the principles of those who carried my bloodline. On my father's side, defiance burned like fire. On my mother's side, principle stood like granite. Together, these legacies gave me both the sword and the compass to face life's battles.

Legacy of My Father's Side

On my father's side, the name Mene Dibayu carried a fierce reputation. Our ancestor, Ato Dibayu Legas, openly defied King Teklehaimanot, refusing to bow to imperial rule. He never carried a royal title because he rejected being beholden to anyone but his people. He fathered twelve children, and from him sprang a vast line of descendants, now numbering in the thousands.

One story about Ato Dibayu has echoed through generations. When he refused to submit, King Teklehaimanot sent an army led by a man who had once been his friend. But Dibayu was forewarned. He and his men prepared for battle and marched out to meet the attack. When the armies clashed, the two leaders found each other in the chaos. Their horses drew close, and Dibayu pulled down the reins of his opponent's horse, forcing him forward. The man's pistol fell to the ground. Dibayu seized it, aimed the weapon, and pointed it at him.

"Dibayu, are you really going to kill me?" the man cried.

"A mother will mourn the loss of a son," Dibayu replied. "I prefer that it be your mother."

Ato Dibayu fired a shot and killed him. The attacking army dispersed and retreated. The king sent more soldiers, but Dibayu and his men melted into the gorge below the plateau, a defensive stronghold and a deathtrap for any invader. Repeatedly, imperial forces failed to root him out.

At last, Teklehaimanot turned to diplomacy. Ato Dibayu was invited to Debre Markos, and the king himself went out to give him an honorary reception. On their way back, they crossed the wide open Wutrn field, a perfect place for pursuit should Dibayu falter. The verbal exchanges rhyme in Amharic giving it a poetic punch.

ንጉሥ ተከለ ሃይማኖት፡ ወጥመዴ ያዘች!

አቶ ዲባዩ፡ አፈነደረች!

"My trap has snared you," the king taunted.

But Dibayu only raised his sword and replied, "Your trap just tripped." He wheeled his horse and galloped away unharmed, untouchable.

The king never pursued him again. From then on, Ato Dibayu ruled Berenta in Gojjam on his own terms, unrecognized by the crown but unchallenged in authority.

This is the legacy my father carried and the legacy I inherited. A lineage of defiance, of standing firm when others bend, of surviving with courage in the face of overwhelming power.

Every child in our family grew up with this story in their veins. Nearly every Mene Dibayu household owns a rifle, and any attack on one family is answered by retribution many times over. Even robbers avoided us, knowing that justice would be swift and merciless. When my father confronted Wubale Tegenu and his armed rebels, he did so with this legacy behind him: the unshakable confidence of a bloodline that never bent to intimidation.

My paternal grandfather Dejazmach Kebede Zeleke. The title bestowed on him posthumously.

That same defiant spirit burned in my grandfather when the Italians invaded Ethiopia for the second time. He was in his early twenties, and my father was still a baby when he marched north with the patriots. The Italians fought with tanks and air power, and when they could not defeat the Ethiopian fighters on the ground, they turned to poison gas. Villages were left charred, families broken, yet my grandfather never surrendered.

He returned home and continued the fight from his home base. His home was burned three times, and still, he rebuilt and continued the fight. His mule, Samun, was wounded in the Battle of Maychew, and that animal became a legend in our family. For years afterward, Samun was the measure of courage: if a man shied away from danger or hesitated to stand his ground, people would say he had shown less courage than the mule.

Our grandfather died from injuries sustained while he was in the line of duty. Haile Selassie visited him at the hospital in Addis Abeba. When he died, his body was flown home in a military helicopter to Yeduha.

The spirit of persistence carried through to my father, who fought his own battles in life without weapons or armies. His legacy to me was not of grand victories but of steady endurance. He taught me that true strength lies not in rushing ahead blindly, but in knowing when to stand firm and when to wait until you are ready.

The Legacy of My Mother's Side

Strength in my bloodline did not come only through defiance. On my mother's side, my grandfather, Mekonnen Adgeh, was the Negadras (head of merchants). Unlike anyone else in the region, he commanded wealth and influence. His caravans of mules and men traveled for weeks, sometimes months, reaching as far as the Sudanese border. He traded, he negotiated, and he brought prosperity back home. His name carried weight, and he was respected, even feared. His sons and grandsons grew strong under his protection, while his daughters and granddaughters carried themselves with the pride of a house rooted in both wealth and reputation.

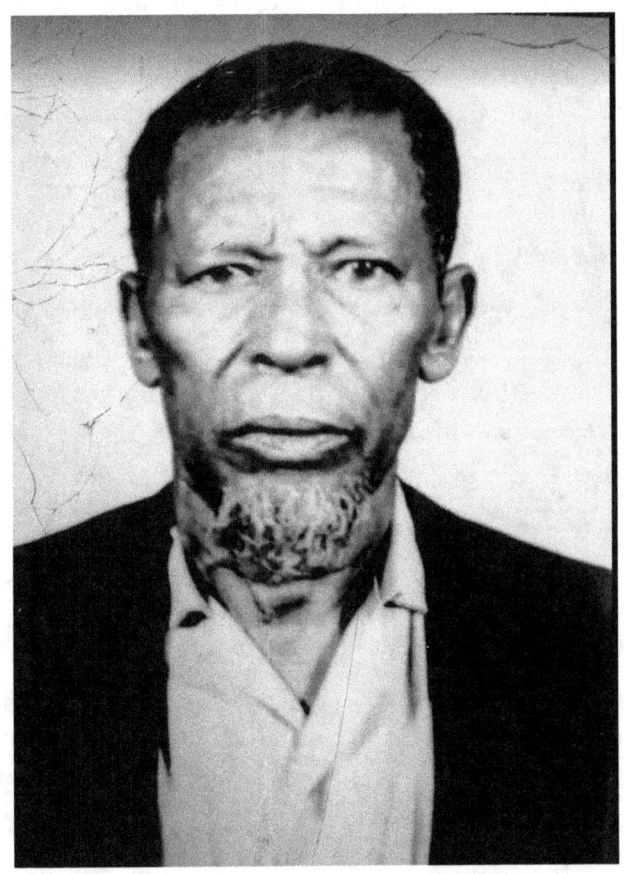

Negadras Mekonen Adgeh our maternal grandfather

Negadras Mekonnen, my grandfather on my mother's side, carried his honor not only in titles, but in action. In Andabet, he faced an influential man who never tired of boasting that no one was greater than him. Their dispute escalated until it reached the highest court in Addis Abeba.

The case dragged on, and expenses piled up. One day, the man announced he would return home before the court reached a decision, claiming he lacked the money to stay. It could have been an easy victory for my grandfather to have his rival concede defeat by leaving the battlefield unfinished.

5

But my grandfather was not satisfied with half-won victories. He reached out to his adversary and offered to cover his expenses. To raise funds, he worked a side job as a tailor. "You will not return to Andabet," he told the man, "Until we properly face each other in court and defeat you."

The rival stayed, supported by the integrity of the very man he had opposed. When the judgment came, he lost the case. The humiliation was so deep he never returned to Andabet.

For my grandfather, the win was not just about the court ruling. It was about principle, about showing that real victory must be earned in the open, not claimed in someone's absence.

The Blend of Two Legacies

These two lineages of warriors on one side, merchants on the other shaped me in profound ways. From my father's family, I inherited courage and the instinct to resist oppression. From my mother's, I inherited resilience, resourcefulness, and the knowledge that prosperity comes to those who dare to reach beyond the familiar.

Together, they gave me a foundation of both fire and wisdom, the strength to fight, and the skill to endure. The blood of warriors and the minds of merchants flowed through me, preparing me for a life that would demand both.

I was five years old with my parents and my sisters. Our father was committed to having pictures taken as much as he could. Smiling at the camera is a recent culture.

My Father's Burden

My father, Shitaye (a term of endearment), inherited not just land and a family name, but also great responsibility. He became a Woreda governor, a role larger in scope than that of a county leader in the United States. It was both a position of authority and one of danger. The memory of the Gojjam Rebellion still stayed. The rebellion was born out of unjust taxation, and those who stood as government figures carried targets on their backs. My grandfather himself had been wounded by a hidden attacker, not because of who he was as a man, but because of what he represented as an official.

My father never forgot this. He knew firsthand what it meant for rulers to be unjust and for ordinary people to rise in anger. Perhaps this was why he left Gojjam for Asela, far from his homeland. Yet fate pulled him back when his father died. He was not the eldest son, but more educated and exposed to government work. The baton became his to carry, not only for his immediate siblings, but also for the extended family and the broader community.

My father was not a man who sought power for its own sake. He carried it because he believed that someone who understood injustice must be the one to resist it at home, he placed a special weight on me. As his eldest child, he reminded me often that my behavior would shape the path of my siblings. When he punished me, he was harsher with me than with the others, justifying it by saying, "Your responsibility is heavier. You must be their example." Even as a boy, I understood his expectations: I was to lead, not simply to live.

When I was around five, my mother told me she would be going away. I did not understand what that meant. Going away for an hour, a day for weeks or what? I remember being in Lumame with my sister and then returning, never imagining that our parents were heading toward divorce. Even if I did, I would not have known what divorce was. Only later did I learn that our mother had gone back to Andabet.

Looking back, I see my father's discipline not as cruelty but as preparation. He demanded more because he believed I could bear more. Leadership, I came to understand, is not about privilege. It is about being willing to be held to a higher standard, even when it feels unfair. That lesson stayed with me through every trial that lay ahead.

The Return of My Mother

Life with our stepmother demanded careful behavior. We were never to let her feel that we preferred our biological mother. My sister Yewul and I wondered often where our mother had gone and why she had left, but those questions had to stay buried. We had a new brother, a new household, and an unspoken rule of silence.

One rainy afternoon, everything changed. My sister and I sat on the floor, our backs pressed against the wall. The door stood open, letting in the only light and fresh air in that small house. Suddenly, through the rain, we saw our mother walking with an umbrella held over her head. The sight made us cry out, "Imeye! Imeye!" Our stepmother rushed to slam the door shut. Minutes passed, stretching into what felt like forever, as we sat in silence, straining to hear any sound, holding onto the hope that she had not vanished again.

When the door finally opened, our mother leapt inside. She had waited cleverly at a neighbor's house next door until the rain slowed down, and the doorway was unguarded. She sat on a wooden box, calm but unyielding. Our stepmother's fury erupted. She raised a wooden pestle high, ready to strike. My mother stood on the box. Her umbrella now gripped like a spear. "This house is mine," she declared. She jumped onto the bed, bouncing on it, shouting, "This bed is mine!" The quarrel escalated until our father intervened.

When the dust settled, my mother handed him a letter. It was from her father, Negadras Mekonen in Andabet. The title Negadras was no mere honorific. It marked him as the leader of trade, a man trusted by authorities to collect taxes, feared by rivals, and respected by all. He had wealth unlike anyone in the region, sending caravans of mules laden with grain as far as the Sudanese border and returning with goods and riches. His family was large and strong, his sons and daughters formidable in both strength and pride.

The letter was not just words. It was a shield. It assured my father that his children would be raised under the protection of this powerful man. My father respected Negadras deeply. Once, when invited to Andabet to take my mother back for a visit, Negadras had even gifted him a pistol. It was a gesture of honor and trust that weighed heavily on him now.

Still, in front of us, our parents fought like enemies. My father clutched my younger sister, pulling one arm, while my mother held the other. They waged a tug-of-war over her body, while I stood frozen, wondering why neither fought for me. My mother handed me a loaf of bread, and I slipped away to eat it in private. When I returned, she was gone again, leaving me without explanation. I was too young to understand the complexities, but old enough to feel the sting. Bread filled my stomach, but not my heart.

Here I am to this day wondering why they did not fight over me. Is it because they did not love me equally? Or did they believe a boy was better raised by his father? Did they divide us like property, and I was simply my father's share? There must have been something they knew then that I still don't know today.

That day burned into my memory a truth about love and survival: adults fight not only for what they want but also for what they believe they can keep. My parents' battle was not about me. It was about the child they thought they could claim. I learned that love could be tangled with power, with fear, and even with survival itself. And I realized that while bread could feed my body, what I hungered for most was belonging.

Lessons in the Dust

Unlike most church-based schools that were held within sacred compounds, mine was in a rented, dusty room in Asela. The smell of damp earth mixed with chalk dust and hung heavy in the air. The benches were uneven, the walls bare, and sunlight leaked faintly through cracks in the mud walls and under the doorway. It was not a grand hall of learning, but to us, it was the place where our journey with the alphabet of both faith and life began.

We learned to read by reciting aloud, voices blending in a rough, uneven rhythm. Each syllable carried the weight of centuries of tradition, echoing the cadence of holy texts. But this was no gentle schooling. The priest walked around us with a whip in his hand, ensuring we stayed focused. The threat of punishment was constant, always hovering in the air like an unseen presence. At times, I could feel his presence behind me before I ever heard his footsteps. The anticipation of discipline was enough to keep me straight-backed and alert.

Fear and reverence went hand in hand. We read and recited, but always with an eye on the imposing figure who circled the room. He was both teacher and enforcer. Though harsh, the method worked. The words etched themselves into our memory, carved deeper by the sting of fear.

These were my earliest lessons not only in reading but in obedience, in resilience, and in the knowledge that learning came with sacrifice. I absorbed not just the written symbols but the rhythm of authority, the weight of silence, and the unspoken truth that survival meant discipline.

Looking back, those days in the dusty room taught me more than letters. They revealed the dual nature of education: both liberating and punishing. The priest's whip reminded me that knowledge was not given freely. It had to be earned through pain, endurance, and humility. Yet, hidden beneath the fear was something else: a seed of determination. I realized then that no matter what the hardship, I wanted to learn. That seed would carry me far beyond Asela, long after the dust in that room settled into memory. faded.

Authority and Legacy

My father had a short marriage with his third wife, and then he married his fourth wife. I came to know Itye, the fourth wife, when we went to her parents' house to visit. At the time, my father and I were living alone. Those visits were courtships, but I was too young to realize. They eventually had a wedding and after some time my brother, Mesfin, was born. Until Mesfin was born, I was the only one in Asela when my father married Itye. I was spoiled then getting attention, I ate special food such as macaroni and spaghetti: the dishes I had never tasted before. I even had a pet cat. But once we moved to Gojjam, everything changed quickly. I was just one among many children, including cousins and other relatives. Most of the people around us were part of my grandfather's extended family. I no longer had my own bed; I slept on the floor with everyone else, on cowhide or sheepskin.

We had two large homes with grass-thatched roofs, surrounded by double fences and guarded. One house was used for preparing and storing food. The other was for receiving guests, with a dining area and my parents' bedroom. The main house was started by my grandfather and completed by my father. The old house contained a fire pit where we gathered in the evenings. The only light came from the fire and a lamp on the wall.

There was no television, only storytelling and folklore. The stories were about hyenas, monkeys, mice, the devil and sometimes about people caught in extramarital affairs. Outside it was dark. So dark that one could not see their own hand in front of them. At times, I had to go to the other house at night, and I remember seeing only a faint flicker of light twinkling in the distance. On moonless nights, the darkness was total. I used to stand in the doorway and wonder when I should make a dash. I worried if the devil would snatch me and take me away. Inspired by the adults' tales, I feared the devil. Once, I claimed to have seen him. The adults, believing a child's heart was pure enough to detect evil, were as frightened as I was. They believed my story.

The town stood on the edge of a cliff overlooking the ravine behind our house and the canyon beyond, where we could hear baboons fighting and making all kinds of sounds. Sometimes, troops of baboons invaded our backyard to eat the corn we planted. At night, we heard hyenas calling in the distance and dogs howling nearby. There was an area set aside to grow hay for the mules and other animals. When the hay grew tall, I loved to walk through it. Occasionally, a quail would burst out of the grass, startling me. Knowing they often nested nearby, I would search for their eggs, sometimes returning home with a few. There were also cactus trees with ripe fruit. Some were within my reach, while others were claimed by the baboons.

The town of Yeduha was completely different from the city of Asela. Men carried rifles and ammunition belts, which we called znar, around their waists. My father, now a government authority, had escorts. At first, people did not like the idea that he was wearing only a jacket like a city man. They wanted to see a more regal dress fit for the position and the culture. They expected him to dress in a gabi (a long white shema) and to carry a zeng (long wooden stuff). I had once walked side by side with him, but now my siblings and I had to walk behind as he went to and from his office. People bowed as they greeted him, even crossing their legs in respect.

A Legacy of Resistance

My father's confidence was not born in isolation; it came from the legacies of those before him. My paternal grandfather had fought against the Italians in the late 1930s, traveling as far as Maychew on foot and riding his mule to resist Mussolini's invasion. When the Ethiopian army was defeated by poison gas and air bombardment, he returned home and waged guerrilla warfare. In Gebsit, where he lived, the Italians burned his house three times, but he never stopped resisting. When they sent planes, my aunt would take the children, including my father, into foxholes until the air raids passed. Down in the canyon below Gebsit, he and other patriots used the narrow paths and cliffs to their advantage. The Italians dared not follow, for they would be easy prey for snipers. He fought with courage and cunning, ensuring his family and neighbors knew that surrender was never an option.

My maternal grandfather, Negadras Mekonen, fought in his own way. As head of merchants, he was wealthier and more influential than anyone in Andabet. He led mule caravans carrying grain as far as the Sudanese border, trading for goods. During the occupation, he sold eggs and ducks to the Italians that the Ethiopians themselves did not eat and in return secured ammunition. Those bullets made their way into the hands of patriots. Where one grandfather wielded the rifle, the other supplied it. Both risked everything to resist.

That legacy flowed into my father, Girazmatch Minyahil. He carried himself with dignity, proud but fair, never one to bend whichever way the wind blew. The Marxist cadres who later overthrew the monarchy would call him feudal, but he had earned his noble title of Girazmatch from Emperor Haile Selassie himself. Authority and resistance were both in his bloodline.

Confrontation with Wubale Tegenu

One day, while my father was in his office, I was outside playing. A man came rushing with a message. He had been sent by a rebel leader named Wubale Tegenu, who commanded a small army of about fifty armed men resting on the outskirts of town. The messenger asked my father's permission for them to enter and speak with him. Permission was granted.

When they entered, they looked menacing, their hair long and wild, coats draped over shoulders, heavy znar belts clinking with ammunition, rifles slung across their chests. I stood to the side, watching with a clear view of my father and these men. Only a couple of police officers were stationed nearby, guarding the small prison next to my father's office.

I saw my father unbutton his coat as he was stepping out of his office. Beneath it, he carried a revolver. I understood what that meant. Then he stepped out tall, proud, head held high. Immediately, all of them bowed low in respect. A wave of pride swept over me as I saw these armed men, two carrying U.S. M1 carbines, Wubale himself with an M1 rifle, and the rest holding assorted weapons from the world wars.

Wubale handed a letter to one of his men, who passed it to my father. Later, my father told us it had been written by a general of the Imperial Guard, who had landed by helicopter nearby and authorized Wubale to collect taxes, perhaps hoping to persuade him to return to peace. My father read the letter, glanced up, and responded with a clear, steady voice.

"You may have been given this letter by some general of the Imperial Guard," he told Wubale, "but I was appointed by His Majesty Haile Selassie. Tax collection is my duty. There can only be one legitimate authority here, and that authority is me. If you disperse your followers and send them back to their farms, I will consider sufficient cooperation. These men following you should go back to their farms. I ask you to immediately disperse your men and return home without stopping anywhere, for any reason."

There were no words of protest, no argument. When my father finished speaking, Wubale and his men bowed deeply, then turned and left, just like that.

But there was more to it than the words. Wubale knew better. He was not standing before just a Woreda administrator. He was standing before a Mene Dibayu, heir to a lineage of men and women who resisted tyranny with both rifle and cunning. Any deviation from my father's order would not only bring the weight of the government down on him, but also the wrath of thousands of fully armed Dibayu descendants who could rise at a moment's notice. His men might not even make it home.

That was the last day Wubale was seen in public until years later in the mid-1970s, when he re-emerged to lead a rebellion against the Derg.

Dates May 25, 1961, Ethiopian calendar translates to June 2, 1969. The letterhead is The Imperial Government of Ethiopia. To Ato (Mr.) Mineyahl Kebede, I am confirming that with his majesty's approval, you are now bestowed the title of Girazmach. With my greetings. Prime Minister Tsehafi Tizaz Aklilu Habte Wold.

Reflection

"That day, as I watched my father face down armed men with nothing but his presence and his words, I realized what true authority meant. It was not simply the office he held, nor even the revolver beneath his coat. It was the legacy of resistance and dignity passed down from both sides of my family. One grandfather fought with bullets in the canyon; another traded with cunning to supply them. My father embodied both legacies.

It was not his weapon that protected him, but the force of his presence, the respect he commanded, and the knowledge that behind him stood both the emperor's authority and the unbreakable unity of the Mene Dibayus. That balance between force and dignity became a lesson etched in me: courage is not only the readiness to fight but the ability to stand firm when all eyes are on you.

For me, that confrontation became more than a story of bravery. It was a lifelong lesson. Years later, when I faced my own trials under the Derg, I would remember that moment. Authority without fear. Authority without compromise. Authority as legacy."

Life in Yeduha and Rebu Gebeya

Life revolved around the rhythm of work and storytelling. Without electricity or television, our nights were filled with tales told by elders, stories of hyenas who tricked monkeys, mice who escaped death, and cautionary tales of betrayal. To me, these stories were not just entertainment but warnings about survival in a world where danger lurked everywhere. The flickering light of the fire and the shadows on the walls made the stories come alive.

Yeduha was no ordinary town. Its people were armed, its fields contested, and its loyalties split between tradition and rebellion. My father walked a narrow line. To his followers, he was a protector; to the rebels, he was a target. To me, he was both father and mystery: stern, dignified, and uncompromising.

My father after the passing of our grandfather. My father took our grandfather's role. Ayaya on the left. Ayawa, 2nd from left, and Itete Yilefu, our aunt.

I learned quickly that life here demanded toughness. No one could survive by softness or by words alone. You had to carry yourself with confidence, know when to speak and when to stay silent, and always, always be ready to defend yourself or your family.

Yeduha shaped me in ways that Asela never could. Here, I learned what it meant to belong to a family with a legacy of power and danger. My father's authority was not just in his title but in his presence, in the way men bowed before him even when they carried rifles. But I also saw the fragility of power. Behind every show of respect was the potential for betrayal.

It was in Yeduha that I began to understand two truths: first, that survival demanded cunning and courage; second, that respect must be earned not by fear alone but by dignity. These lessons would stay with me for life, guiding me when I later faced my own crossroads of danger, exile, and leadership.

In elementary school, I was full of energy and eager to take part in everything. Coming from the city, I was outgoing and confident. My father's position as the highest authority in town, and my grandfather's noble reputation, seemed to cast a spotlight on me. Teachers and classmates noticed me more, and I thrived in that attention.

I became a drummer in school parades, pounding rhythms that carried lines of students through the dusty streets. I created sound effects during drama performances, making horses gallop and thunder roar using nothing more than wood, tin, or my own voice. School was not only about reading and arithmetic, but also a stage where I discovered my voice.

Parents' Day – Pride and Cunning

Parents' Day was always a highlight at school, filled with shows, dramas, and competitions. That year, I found myself in two events that revealed very different sides of me.

The first was a contest of strength. Another boy my size, the son of a police officer, and I were chosen to face off. We lay face down in the dirt, our ankles tied with a belt, and between us sat a bottle of soda, the prize. Around the field, parents watched, including my father who sat in the center on a high seat because of his rank, and my opponent's father on the sideline.

When the count began, the other boy immediately started dragging me across the field. For a moment, I felt the weight of shame rising in my chest and the humiliation I would carry for weeks if I lost. I could not bear for my father to watch me defeated, not in front of the town where he was the highest authority.

Just then, I spotted a deep crack in the hard, dry clay beneath me. I reached out, grabbed hold, and let my opponent wear himself out. I bided my time, saving my strength. When I felt him weakening, I pulled with everything I had, again and again, until I dragged him across the line. I grabbed the soda bottle, and as I raised it, I heard my father's laughter echo across the field. That sound was the approval I craved. I had made him proud and secured my reputation as a winner.

Later that day, I was also in the spaghetti-eating contest. The rules were simple: finish the most pasta in the shortest time. While the others stuffed themselves furiously, faces smeared with sauce, I chose a different path. I twirled the spaghetti slowly, savoring each bite.

At first, the crowd was confused. But soon they began laughing and nudging each other: "That's exactly what I would have done!" By the time the contest ended, I had eaten far less than the others, but I had won something greater: the audience's admiration and the simple joy of the food. I didn't follow the rules, but I had stolen the show. The eating contest was never what impressed our community. Physical stamina was admired, but neither overeating nor eating fast.

That Parents' Day taught me two lessons I carried throughout my life: sometimes victory comes from grit, endurance, and refusing to let go. Other times, it comes from thinking differently, ignoring the noise, and winning people's respect on your own terms.

Academically, I excelled. After ranking first in third grade, I was allowed to skip a year, completing both third and fourth grades together. In fifth grade, we had to memorize and recite English poems under strict conditions. One of them has never left me, even fifty years later:

> *Where are you going, my little goat?*
> *I am going to the market to buy a new coat.*
> *A coat for a goat? Can a goat have a coat?*
> *We people laugh at a goat with a coat.*

I recited it proudly, though my voice trembled at first. Some teachers were encouraging, but others were harsh. Once, I made a wooden pistol for a handcraft project. Instead of guiding me, the teacher scolded me and dismissed it as "a destructive tool." Still, I pressed forward.

By the time I was eleven, I had finished elementary school. But our small town offered no education beyond the sixth grade. My father had to decide:

should I continue my studies in Bichena or Debre Markos? A relative recommended Debre Markos, praising its foreign teachers and the chance to study in English. My father agreed, and so at age twelve, I moved to Debre Markos to live with Ato Taye Alemu.

Chapter 2 – Beyond Elementary School

Once I finished elementary school, life took on a different rhythm. At just twelve years old, my father took me to Debre Markos and entrusted me to the care of Ato Taye. I still remember my father's face as he left me there filled with pride, resolve, and quiet worry. He wanted me to have an education, something more than what the countryside could offer, but it meant leaving the comfort of family and stepping into a harder kind of independence.

There were no blankets, only the thin layer of fabric on my body, but I never complained. I had shelter. I had food. And above all, I had the opportunity to attend school. That, I knew, was worth more than comfort.

At night, when the house was quiet and I lay on my mat, I sometimes felt the weight of loneliness. The warmth of my family was far away. I missed my father's gentle voice, my siblings' laughter, and the familiar rhythm of home. But each morning I rose with determination. I told myself this was the price of education, the sacrifice that would one day lift me higher.

It was not luxury, but it was shelter. It was not comfort, but it was dignity. And in that corner of the dining room, with books for a pillow and discipline as my blanket, I learned one of life's greatest lessons: survival is not just about enduring hardship, but about carrying it with purpose. Those nights built my resilience. They trained me to see dignity in small things, strength in silence, and pride in perseverance.

Life with Ato Taye

This was not my first encounter with him. Years earlier, Ato Taye had been the principal of Yeduha Elementary School, where my journey began. Now, he was principal in Abma, a suburb of Debre Markos, and once again, our paths crossed. More than a teacher, he was the godfather of my youngest brother, Yohanes.

My father trusted him, and so I was placed in his care. My place was simple: a grass mat unrolled in the corner of the dining area. At night, I used my clothes as a pillow, and in the morning, I rolled the mat back up. It was shelter, and I accepted it.

Ato Taye was sharp and observant. He praised my maturity and nicknamed me "Aba Zinah," a title carrying both affection and expectation. I wanted to live up to it.

Still, life in his home had its challenges. Another boy was staying with us, recovering from a broken thigh. One evening, he disturbed me as I worked on my homework. When I asked Ato Taye to intervene, he refused. Frustrated, I lashed out and kicked the boy, who screamed in pain. In an instant, Ato Taye rose to chase me, but I bolted into the night, disappearing into the darkness.

I wasn't proud of the outburst, but I was proud of standing my ground. My father had raised me to be strong and unwilling to be trampled. That silent approval was enough for me.

My Father and the Outlaw Alemu Wonde

While I was away in school that same year, my father transferred from Yeduha to Rebu Gebeya as Woreda Administrator. He was now only 28 kilometers away (four-hour walk) away from me which was much closer than distant Yedwuha. His priority, as always, was peace. Soon he heard rumors of Alemu Wonde, an outlaw who had terrorized the region for eighteen years. Alemu robbed travelers, refused to pay taxes, and lived beyond the reach of government authority.

Determined to resolve the matter, my father sent a message through a man who knew Alemu: come to peace, lay down your arms, and live within the law. But the messenger never returned. The message was clear. No response meant Alemu had refused.

My father, Girazmach Mineyahil Kebede, when he was the Woreda Governor of Snan Chero Woreda with his office and residence in Robu Gebeya. This picture was taken by a UN employee, Mr. Yuki of Japan that was vaccinating the population to eradicate smallpox. He had translators and I sometimes helped the best way I could. I was 12 at the time in 7th grade.

My father with his escorts when he was the governor in Dbate, Metekel.

My father sought reinforcements. The police sent forty armed officers with a mounted machine gun. My father also recruited trusted volunteers from the community. Before setting out, he hosted them for dinner, then revealed the mission. Each man swore an oath by stepping across three loaded rifles laid on the floor, saying:

ይህ ቢስት ይህ አይሳተኝ፦ ይህ ቢስት ይህ አይሳተኝ፦

"If this one miss, may this one not miss me. If this one miss, may the next one not miss me."

It was a solemn vow: betrayal would mean death at the hands of one's own comrades.

Before daybreak, they marched northward, keeping low until they reached Alemu's stronghold. Surrounded, Alemu burst out, firing a long Mannlicher rifle. He retreated into a bamboo thicket, but a storm of bullets shredded the cover. Farmers loyal to Alemu fired back, calling for reinforcements. The police unleashed the machine gun, a show of overwhelming force.

Outnumbered and outgunned, Alemu surrendered. He was brought before my father for a stern stare-down. Alemu was furious, yet also proud. He served three years in prison. Later, as my father and I walked in town, we passed Alemu on the road. To my surprise, Alemu bowed deeply in respect. My father told me that Alemu had thanked him for ending his life as an outlaw, freeing him from fear and giving him a chance to live in peace.

Through strength, justice, and dignity, my father had turned a menace into a man. He gave Rebu Gebeya peace.

Reflection

This chapter of my life was a lesson in contrast. At school, I learned to find my voice in poems, parades, and performances. In Ato Taye's home, I learned the value of discipline, dignity, and the hard edge of independence. And through my father, I witnessed the power of true leadership.

It was not weapons alone that subdued Alemu Wonde, but the aura of respect my father carried in his authority as both a Woreda Administrator and a Mene Dibayu. Behind him stood not only the emperor's appointment but the loyalty of family and tribe. He turned lawlessness into peace without losing his dignity.

From him, I learned that courage is not just about fighting. It is about standing firm when all eyes are on you, carrying yourself with honor even in the face of danger. That lesson stayed with me and began shaping the man I was becoming.

A New Shelter

After my time with Ato Taye ended, my father arranged for me to live with my aunt, closer to the school. He provided food, and she offered me shelter. But "shelter" in those days did not mean comfort. My bed was a wooden bench. I waited each night until the house went quiet, then stretched out on the bench, free at last to rest. I hung my jacket on a nail in the wall, using my few books and clothes as a pillow.

It was not luxury, but it was mine. Unlike the crowded cowhide mats of earlier years, this bench was my own small territory, a reminder that survival often meant claiming the simplest corner of space.

My aunt's husband, a police chief, often came home with copies of the government newspaper Police and Progress. He must have received it free, but instead of reading it, he used it to cover the walls. The entire room became a patchwork of newsprint, some sheets sideways and others upside down. At night, as I lay on my bench, I studied the walls. Even though they were propaganda, I tried to read between the lines, to glimpse some truth hidden within the lies.

One year, Pepsi ran a promotion. Under each bottle cap was a drawing, and certain drawings won prizes. I peeled one cap and discovered I had won a wristwatch. It was my treasure, proof of luck and status. But when I asked my aunt's husband to hold it for safekeeping, he later refused to return it. Instead, he wore it himself, claiming the winning bottle cap had belonged to his son. I was crushed. How could a man whose profession was to uphold law and order rob a boy of his prize? That injustice burned into me.

Life with my cousins was lively, but not without conflict. Once, I fought with a girl during recess. I was winning until her older sister joined in. Outnumbered, I was soon rescued by another cousin, a proud Mene

Dibayu, who evened the fight. When the teachers discovered us, the three of us were punished. I claimed self-defense, but the teachers insisted I bring a parent. I refused. My father was too far away, and my aunt already thought me troublesome. Besides, if my father found out, his punishment would be worse than anything the school could devise.

So I accepted the school's punishment: carrying heavy building stones from the school's entrance to the principal's office window and back again. Back and forth until my arms and back ached. Yet I carried those stones with pride. They were a burden I accepted in exchange for my dignity. Better to shoulder the weight than bring shame to my family name.

Reflection

Looking back, I see that my new shelter was not simply a bench beneath papered walls. It was a classroom of life itself. From the injustice of the stolen watch, I learned that power can corrupt even those meant to protect. From the school fight and punishment, I learned that dignity sometimes demands silent endurance. Carrying stones was not just discipline. It was a lesson in accepting hardship without losing face.

Ethiopian schools of the time were shaped by both church tradition and modern discipline, where strict punishments were considered part of molding character. Children were also judged by their family names, their lineage as much as their own deeds. For me, being the son of a Woreda administrator and grandson of warriors and merchants, every action was measured against that reputation.

Yet this chapter taught me something deeper: a boy could begin to shape his own identity even within the walls of propaganda and under the weight of punishment. I discovered how to read between the lines, how to stand firm without calling on others to fight my battles, and how to endure injustice without surrendering hope.

This was the beginning of my resilience. Each stone I carried, each night I lay staring at those paper-covered walls, prepared me for the far heavier burdens that awaited in the years of terror and exile to come.

Moving Closer to My Mother

When my father was transferred again, this time to Bahir Dar, the city by the great Lake Tana, my life changed in ways I did not expect. Bahir Dar was nothing like Debre Markos. It was a city with a vast, glittering lake that seemed to stretch endlessly, though its shoreline was jagged with rocks and tangled with papyrus reeds. There were no soft sandy beaches, only sharp stones and marshes where water birds nested. Sometimes I went to the lake to wash my clothes. Other times, driven by curiosity, I borrowed a small papyrus boat left by the shore. I paddled out, not to fish, but to reach places no one else bothered to go. There I found fruit trees, their ripe fruit dropping into the water and floating within my reach. It felt like the lake itself was handing me a gift.

For the first time since my earliest years, all my brothers and sisters were together under one roof. My older brother had joined us, studying at the high school in Bahir Dar, and my younger siblings were still in primary school. We grew as a unit, sometimes playful, sometimes mischievous, but always bound by the sense that we were moving through life together.

One of the most remarkable experiences of this period was traveling with my father on official trips. I carried his paperwork, making myself useful, but more importantly, I observed him in action. Watching him handle disputes, manage officials, and make decisions left a deep impression on me. It was my first education in leadership not from books but from witnessing authority exercised with firmness and dignity.

My father's title at this time was Bahrdar Zuria Woreda Governor. In Amharic, Zuria means "surrounding," and his jurisdiction was over the lands encircling the city, while the city itself was under a mayor. His office, however, was located in Bahir Dar proper. During the reign of Haile Selassie, officials from woreda level upward were called "governors," a term that carried prestige and authority. But under the Derg, that title was abandoned. "Governor" carried a feudal connotation, suggesting superiority and aristocratic dominance that clashed with the Derg's socialist ideology. Titles were stripped down to sound more egalitarian, even as the regime itself ruled with an iron fist. At the time, Bahir Dar was expanding rapidly, destined to become a modern metropolitan city. For that to happen, the surrounding lands had to be incorporated into its growth. My father was at the center of this delicate process.

His office in Bahir Dar was near the lake, and often, while he worked, I slipped to the shoreline to watch the waves roll in. The papyrus plants swayed gently in the breeze, their shadows rippling on the water, and I would lose myself in the rhythm of lake life. On one trip, I was able to visit the Zege Peninsula, a place I had always dreamed of seeing. With its monasteries hidden in thick forests and its sense of timelessness, Zege seemed a world apart.

At the time, my father's most important responsibility was the incorporation of eighteen debir ager (farming communities, each centered around its church) into the city of Bahir Dar. Traditionally, each debir was a self-contained unit with its own small governance structure and deep ties to its land. But Bahir Dar was growing, and the future demanded expansion. The task was controversial, since the eighteen debir lands technically lay across the Blue Nile in Begemdir province. Gojjam, our home, was always considered to be all the land surrounded by the Blue Nile. Incorporating lands beyond the river stretched that definition, and my father had to navigate both politics and local resistance.

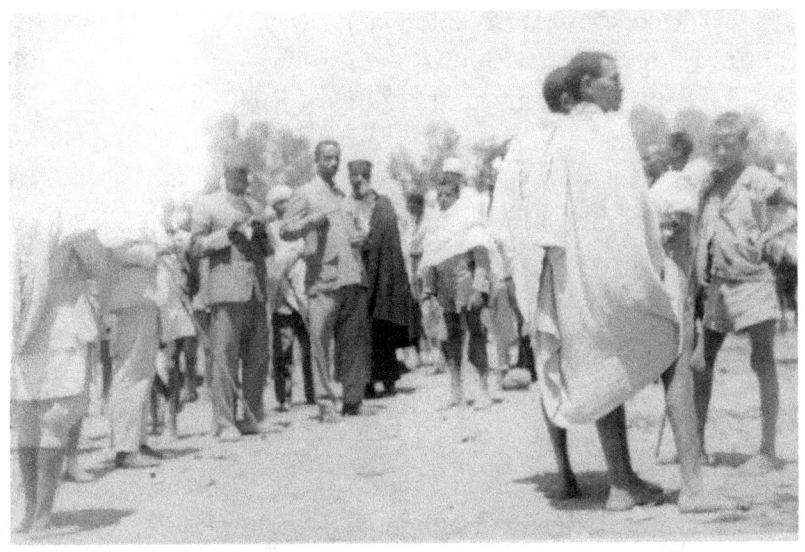

My father stood to the left of the priest, and I am on the right, wearing shorts and a gabi. I carried my father's files while he campaigned in the countryside and held meetings with the people. I was 13 at the time.

One year, the city's waterline broke near our neighborhood. The municipality did nothing to fix it, no matter how many complaints were raised. My siblings and I saw the puddled water and decided to make use of it. We dug into the soil, planted seeds, and grew a vegetable patch on the wet ground. When the authorities heard that children were farming around their leaking pipeline, they finally came and repaired it. For us, it was a small victory: children forcing officials into action with nothing more than our resourcefulness.

Behind the Bahir Dar stadium, people from Zegé Peninsula and other nearby areas sold firewood and charcoal in small markets. Papyrus boats lay stacked on the shore, abandoned until their owners returned. It was from this market that I borrowed the boat to gather fruit. Looking back, I realize how daring it was, paddling out alone on the waters of Tana without knowing how deep or dangerous they might be. But at the time, I felt only adventure.

My mother lived about thirty kilometers away, and she often came to Bahir Dar for shopping or to visit us. On one such visit, she gave me money to buy bread for myself and my younger sisters. Each evening after school, I stopped at the bakery. The loaves were fresh, still warm, and the smell alone made it impossible to wait. I always ate my piece on the way home. By the time I arrived, my sisters were already asleep. I would gently place the warm bread on their foreheads, waking them with the heat. They smiled and grumbled, half-annoyed, half-amused. It was my mischievous way of telling them, "I thought of you."

A Boy with Ideas

As I grew into my early teens, my curiosity about the world widened, and with it came a restless desire to do more than simply pass the days. My mother gave me freedom, trusting that I would not waste it. I was neither idle nor destructive. Instead, I looked for ways to learn, to test myself, and to create something out of nothing.

When school was closed, I often spent time in front of our house, watching the movements of people and goods. One day, a truck was being loaded with grain bound for Asmara. The driver was my cousin, Belay Yismaw, the same cousin who, six years later, would give me a ride from Dejen to Addis Abeba, setting me on the path toward safety and in safety and in comfort while hiding in plain sight. At the time, I only saw the excitement of a truck heading to a faraway city. A year later, I joined my cousins Adebabay and Dagnachew, riding on our uncle, Aba Birru's truck all the way to Asmara. For a teenage boy, that trip felt like crossing into another world.

But I was not just an observer. I was always thinking about how to turn small opportunities into something bigger. One day, I asked my mother for ten cents, enough to buy fish and a few more coins for a bus ride. I went to Gumara and discovered fish being sold for a single cent each. I bought, brought them home, cleaned and fried them, and asked my mother to sell them at her hotel. Each fish sold for twenty-five cents. On each one-cent cost, I made a twenty-four-cent gross profit. It was my first real lesson in

32

enterprise and how an idea and a little effort could multiply into something greater.

Another time, I found my brother's bicycle locked and unused, the key taken with him. For two days, I worked on it until I managed to open the lock. I used wires pulled out of an old umbrella to pick the lock. I took the bike to the street and rode it proudly at first, but soon I saw something more. A bicycle was a rare treasure in Hamusit, and many boys wanted the chance to ride it. So, I began renting it out. That bicycle became my first business venture, a way to turn curiosity into opportunity.

These were small things, but they shaped me. Even as a boy, I was learning the value of imagination, persistence, and enterprise. My mother's trust gave me the space to explore, and my own determination turned play into purpose. Looking back, those early experiments with fish and bicycles were more than just childhood adventures. They were the seeds of resilience and creativity that would carry me through far greater challenges later in life.

Reflection

Living in Bahir Dar during this stage of my youth taught me about power, growth, and the responsibility that comes with both. Watching my father serve as Bahrdar Zuria Woreda Governor showed me that authority was not simply about giving orders. It was also about balancing tradition, justice, and vision. His work to incorporate the eighteen debir ager into Bahir Dar's future expansion revealed how governance is never only about today. It is about tomorrow, about shaping space for a community to grow.

For me, those days by the lake were more than childhood memories. They were quiet lessons. As I carried my father's paperwork and trailed beside him, I saw the way decisions shaped lives. I saw how titles and structures changed from the "governors" of Haile Selassie's time to the stripped-down administrators of the Derg, yet the true weight of leadership came not from a title but from the respect one could command. My father's authority was rooted in both: the legitimacy of office and the reputation of his family's legacy.

Even the lake itself felt like a teacher. In the swaying papyrus, the drifting Water Berry (ዶቅማ) (Syzygium guineense) fruit, and the papyrus boats resting on the shore, I learned about resourcefulness, patience, and risk. When I paddled out alone, I did not only gather fruit. I gathered courage, daring to explore the unknown.

And with my mother's visits, bringing money for bread and small tokens of her care, I began to realize that love was not only in words or presence. Sometimes, love was in the warm bread pressed against my sisters' faces at night, waking them with laughter.

I had small adventures of a restless boy, but they taught me lessons that would last a lifetime: how to see possibilities where others saw limitations, how to take risks, and how to create something out of almost nothing. The same instincts that guided me with fish and bicycles would later guide me through far more serious challenges when the stakes were no longer a few coins, but my very survival.

Looking back, I see that Bahir Dar was a place where two worlds converged: the world of authority and politics that my father navigated, and the world of childhood curiosity and play that shaped me. It was here I began to sense that I stood between two inheritances of my father's dignity and power, my mother's care and cunning, and that one day, I would need to carry both.

Searching for Stability

By ninth grade, I returned to Debre Markos with my younger sister, Yewul. She had completed sixth grade, and like many children from smaller towns, she now needed to come to a larger city to continue her schooling. Together, we moved from place to place, always relying on relatives.

At first, we stayed with Itye Alemitu, my godfather's ex-wife. She was kind, joyful, and easy to live with. My sister helped her with chores while I played with friends after school. Later, we were given a room by another relative attached to a typing school. To reach it, we had to cut through a crowded classroom, so instead we used a window to sneak in and out.

Eventually, we lived with our aunt, Itete Molla, one of the kindest women I have ever known. She rented us a side extension of her house for two Birr a month. For our meals, we relied on a qelabit (ቀላቢት): a woman who cooked and served meals to students under a verbal agreement in which we paid once a month. Most of her customers were students from smaller towns, and sometimes single men without a wife or maid to cook for them. Kelabit in Amharic literally means "the one who feeds," and for students like us, far away from our parents, it was more than just food. It was comfort, routine, and proof that such a role was needed in our society. In Ethiopia at that time, men rarely cooked; feeding students was both a livelihood and a service.

Over time, my sister began to cook for us. She prepared shiro wot regularly, and I regret teasing her by calling it "doke," a word dismissive and ungrateful. At the time, I didn't appreciate the effort she made to keep us fed. Now, I see clearly that she carried a burden far beyond her years.

These were unsettled years, marked by constant moving, but we never ran out of family willing to shelter us. Still, Ethiopia itself was changing, and so was my fate. By the time I reached eleventh grade, the political turmoil that had been simmering for years boiled over. Teachers and students alike were swept into underground movements. Fear and suspicion crept into every classroom. And soon, violence would step directly through the doors of our school.

My younger sister Yewul on the left, I am in the middle 5th from the left or right. My best friend, Bayush, on the right, and Addisu, 3rd from right.

Reflection

This chapter of my life taught me that stability is not about where you sleep or even who puts food on the table. It is about the bonds you build and the gratitude you carry. My sister, still a child herself, shouldered a responsibility she didn't deserve, and I regret the times I failed to honor that. Her simple meals of shiro wot were more than food. They were an expression of sacrifice and love. What I once dismissed as "the same thing over and over" was, in truth, her way of ensuring that we survived.

The kelabit women, too, were part of this lesson. They filled a cultural gap, ensuring that students like us did not go hungry while chasing an education far from home. In their small kitchens, with wood fires and iron pots, they carried forward the unseen work that kept a generation of young people alive during uncertain times. They represented something deeply Ethiopian: a community always finds a way to feed its children, even when the state has failed.

Looking back, I see now that resilience in Ethiopia has always been built on such acts of love and service. Families take in relatives, communities step in for parents, and neighbors share food with strangers. Even in the most unstable times, there was a net held together from kinship and culture. Without it, I would not have survived.

At the same time, the instability of our living arrangements mirrored the instability of Ethiopia itself. Just as we moved from house to house, the entire nation seemed to be shifting under our feet with political alliances breaking, violence brewing, and trust fading away. Yet even as the country's leaders failed, ordinary people held the line. My sister cooking shiro wot each day, the kelabit women feeding students, and my aunt renting us a room for two birr a month, and these were the foundations of survival.

I learned then that resilience does not come from governments or armies; it comes from families, from sisters who cook when they should be playing, from women who feed strangers, from communities that refuse to let children starve. It was this resilience with sacrifice, small kindnesses, and unspoken obligations, that sustained me, and it remains one of the deepest lessons of my life.

The Night of the Missing Mule

When I was seventeen, I went to my father's home in Rebu Gebeya during a school break. My friend Addisu came along. One afternoon while we were out, we returned to find the maid in a state of nervousness.

"Someone came and took the mule," she told us.

"What do you mean?" I asked, my heart tightening.

She looked down, ashamed. "I don't know who it was. I was too shy to ask. And... they also took Wubetu."

The words struck me like a thunderbolt. Our mule, Shekle, was gone and with it, my younger brother.

It was the time when killings were common in the big cities. A story I had once heard echoed in my mind: criminals sometimes eliminate witnesses after being seen. The thought of Wubetu in danger filled me with dread. Being the eldest child in my father's absence, I knew I could not simply wait and hope for the best.

The maid pointed in the direction they had gone. Addisu and I grabbed our sticks and started walking west. Night fell quickly, and we found ourselves at the edge of a raging river. The water roared in the dark, and without light, we feared stepping in would mean drowning. We slept cold and uneasy on the riverbank, waiting for dawn.

At first light, we crossed the river and kept walking. Hours later, we saw a road and followed it north, without any clear destination, only determination. Eventually, a sign appeared: Amaneul. By then, we had walked more than thirty kilometers.

As we entered the town, my heart jumped. In the distance, tied outside a house, stood Shekle, our mule.

Addisu and I raised our sticks and moved close to the wall of the house. Inside, I could see my brother Wubetu sitting comfortably, drinking tea with a man we recognized, a visitor who often came to our home.

We stepped inside and demanded to know why they had come and why the mule was there. They looked up, startled, but calm. The man explained: our father had asked him to bring the mule to this town on that very day, because my father would be passing through with a guest. When the man arrived, Wubetu had insisted on coming along.

Soon after, my father himself arrived. When we explained what had happened, and why we had followed, he looked at me with pride. He knew that, even at seventeen, I had shown the courage and responsibility to act when my family and our belongings seemed to be in danger.

That night taught me something I carried through the rest of my life: when something seems wrong, do not sit and wait but, act.

Climbing the Choke Mountains

When my father served as Woreda Administrator in Sinan Chero, we often traveled between there and Debre Markos. I grew up hearing a phrase repeatedly, almost like poetry: the Choke Mountains are unreachable.

ከጮቄ ተራራ ከጥጉ ይርቃ

ወይ አለመታደል መጣሁ ተመልሼ

Their four jagged peaks loomed on the horizon, cloaked in mist and legend, as if they were meant only to be admired from afar.

One day, as a restless teenager, I decided I would climb the tallest of them. I could not accept that something so near could be called impossible. Word spread quickly, and other boys joined me after hearing my plan. Instead of discouraging us, my father surprised me. He placed in my hands his prized military-grade binoculars, the ones he valued dearly, and told me to take them with me.

We set off on foot, the climb taking nearly three hours. The air grew thinner, the trail steeper, but step by step we reached the summit, twelve thousand feet above sea level. At the top, I raised the heavy binoculars to my eyes, expecting to see far-off towns or perhaps the edge of the earth itself. Instead, the horizon remained faint and hazy, hidden behind layers of cloud and distance.

We came home tired but triumphant. We had proven the mountain could be climbed, that the unreachable could, in fact, be reached. For me, that climb was more than an adventure. It was a declaration. I was not the kind to accept limits written into old sayings. I was not the kind to watch from below and wonder. Even then, I understood that some things can only be known by trying, and that every horizon, however faint, is worth the climb.

Chapter 3 – Shadows of the Red Terror

The country was unraveling before my eyes. By the late 1970s, Ethiopia had become a battlefield of competing revolutions and foreign invasion. The Derg, led by Mengistu Haile Mariam, ruled with an iron fist and Soviet backing, intent on building a regime modeled after the Bolsheviks. They promised equality and justice, but what they delivered was fear, executions, and mass graves.

The Derg was under attack on nearly every front. In the north, the Ethiopian Democratic Union (EDU) waged war in Gojjam and Begemder. In Eritrea, the EPLF and ELF fought fiercely, joined by the TPLF in Tigray, who coordinated guerrilla attacks and shared strategy with the Eritreans. Inside the cities, including Addis Ababa, the EPRP organized underground resistance and strikes, inspiring hope among students but drawing merciless retaliation. From the southeast, Somalia invaded, pushing 300 kilometers into Ethiopia from the Ogaden and nearly 700 kilometers from the south. And within the capital itself, Mengistu barely escaped an assassination attempt.

Instead of crumbling, the Derg doubled down. Inspired by Stalin, Mao, and Pol Pot, Mengistu unleashed Ethiopia's own version of the Great Purge: The Red Terror. His message was brutal: "Death to the counterrevolutionaries!" Walls were splashed with slogans written in blood; bodies were left on the streets as warnings. Neighbors were forced to spy on neighbors, children on parents. Even neutrality was branded as guilt. Officials announced openly that "a neutral person is punished twice, once from each side."

By this time, my father had already been arrested. To the cadres, he was a symbol of the old world, a man with dignity, carrying the title of Girazmach, bestowed by Emperor Haile Selassie. That alone made him suspect. Haile Selassie himself was gone, suffocated in his cell in August 1975, and in 1992 his remains were found, buried under a toilet in the palace. Seventy high-ranking government officials had been executed without trial. By 1977, the Red Terror had attacked and killed up to 980,000 people. It was clear: if they could kill an emperor, what hope was left for ordinary men like my father or for me?

The Red Terror came crashing into my own life most vividly during my high school years in Debre Markos. Schools became recruiting grounds for loyalty, arenas for fear. One day, we were ordered to assemble in the central square of the campus. The man who presided over us was Lieutenant Eshetu Alemu, second-in-command to Melaku Tefera, the infamous butcher of Gonder. Eshetu had been sent to Gojjam to carve his own legacy of blood. Later, he would face justice in The Hague, convicted of crimes against humanity. But on that day, he was untouchable, drunk with power, determined to terrify us into submission.

They began with speeches and propaganda so familiar it washed over us like background noise. But soon the true purpose emerged: confessions. Students were dragged to the front and told to admit their ties to underground movements. Some accused others to save themselves. Others broke under pressure. Betrayal became survival, and fear turned classmates into informants.

I stood silent. I would not play their game. quietly, I tore my student ID apart, shredding it into tiny pieces and chewing the scraps so that no one could reconstruct it. My resolve was firm: if they came for me, I would resist, even if it meant death. I studied the soldiers around me, rifles in hand, and thought through how I might snatch one if pressed. At eighteen, I had no illusions left but only the determination to live or die with dignity.

When the assembly finally ended, we were warned: the hunt would continue at night. They would come into our homes, drag us from our beds. As we left campus, the tension weighed on every step. My sister and I walked quickly, saying little. That day, I had survived by instinct, cunning, and sheer will. But survival was no longer enough. The Red Terror had turned Ethiopia into a place where even children were forced to calculate life and death.

Reflection

This period was the threshold where my innocence ended. I was no longer simply a student. I had become a marked person in a war between rulers and the ruled. What the Derg failed to understand was that every killing, every humiliation, every staged confession only deepened our resolve.

I learned two lessons that never left me:

1. Fear is their weapon, but dignity is our shield. Even if stripped of titles, wealth, or freedom, a person who stands firm cannot be truly broken.

2. Silence can be a form of resistance. Sometimes the most powerful act is not to speak, not to betray, not to confess, but to hold your ground even when the world demands your submission.

This was the world that shaped me. And this was the world I vowed to outlast.

Defiance in Silence

If the wrong attitude could get me thrown into a police cell for three days, beaten, and threatened with execution... If one single family letter containing trivial speculation could earn me eleven days in jail... then what would happen if they discovered that I supported the opposition, that I despised a military dictatorship?

The killings throughout the country made one thing clear: I could not expect mercy or understanding from this regime.

By this time, my father had already been arrested without explanation. He was a man of dignity and carried an aura of respect. He was not the kind that flowed in whatever direction the wind blew. The Marxist cadres despised him as a feudal leader. He held the title of Girazmach, a mark of nobility bestowed on him by Emperor Haile Selassie himself. But Haile Selassie was no longer there to protect men like my father. The emperor had been deposed, imprisoned, and in August 1975 was likely suffocated in his cell. Seventy government officials had already been executed without trial. Years later, in 1992, the emperor's remains were discovered under a toilet in the palace, a grim confirmation of the cruelty of those days.

One by one, students were pressured to admit their involvement in clandestine organizations and to denounce others. They warned us that if we did not confess, they had ways of finding out. A few students went up to the stage and spoke. I could not tell whether they were telling the truth or simply trying to save themselves and gain mercy by getting others to confess.

The atmosphere grew heavier. Students began naming names, bringing secrets into the open. Fear twisted the crowd. Then they asked us to break into smaller groups according to the kebele (neighborhood association) we lived in, making it easier to track and arrest us later.

I was only eighteen, with no money, no network, no resources, but only my family and my younger sister, who lived with me. But I also had courage, and I had already learned: survival was not about compliance. It was about resolving.

Reflection

That day was a turning point. I had seen enough to understand that silence was its own form of resistance. By refusing to speak, by refusing to give them names, I chose dignity over fear. I learned that sometimes survival means defiance, not shouting slogans, but standing firm in silence when the world around you trembles.

Eshetu Alemu and men like him believed terror could crush us into obedience. But inside me, terror forged something different: clarity. I would not wait for them to knock on my door. I would take the next step, write my own script, and choose my own path of defiance.

Vanished In Thin Air

In Ethiopia, city dwellers and countryside people dress very differently. Someone my age from a farmer's family looked nothing like a high school student. I had a wristwatch my father had given me two years earlier, wore Levi jeans and leather shoes, and my hair had grown into an afro. If I walked out of town like that, I wouldn't last a day. Someone would stop me or report me to the authorities. Word had spread that students who opposed the military junta were being arrested and taken away.

I asked my sister to cut my hair. All we had were dull scissors. The result was uneven, even worse than before. My hair in that state would draw unwanted attention. So, we found a black hat to cover it. Black was customarily worn in mourning, and I decided it would help disguise me. I went barefoot, wore a gabi, and carried a stick, trying to look like a farmer. From a distance, the disguise worked; up close, it might still give me away.

The night passed without incident. No one came looking for me, and I felt a small sense of relief. At dawn, I quietly stepped outside. My sister was nervous and worried. She didn't know what else to do for me. She loved sugar and offered some, showing how badly she felt.

As I neared the edge of town, I saw two men patrolling. Curfew was enforced in many streets. I immediately crouched in the bushes, waiting for them to pass. Once it was safe, I began walking toward Yeboqla, where my fourth mother's family lived. Her brother, once my classmate, had dropped out to become a farmer. I knew going somewhere, anywhere, was better than surrendering.

The footpath was dried clay, cracked into clods and broken by animal hooves. Walking barefoot, it felt like gravel, so I carefully sidestepped onto soft grass to avoid the sharp pain. After a few hours, I arrived at a large settlement and suspected it was Yeboqla. A man confirmed it, then directed me to Mengesha's home.

Mengesha came out to greet me. He recognized me immediately but looked puzzled by my appearance. I explained that I was going to Berenta,

44

my father's birthplace, to collect supplies, and that I didn't feel safe in my usual clothing because someone might mistake me for fleeing the government. He invited me to lunch, then pointed me toward Kuyi, where more relatives lived.

Eventually, I reached a village full of huts. I asked again where I was and learned it was Deboza, near Kuyi. I introduced myself as the son of Girazmatch Minyahil and asked to rest for the night. A woman overheard and immediately saw that something was wrong. She noticed my bare feet, beat her chest, and cried, but she took my hand and led me into her hut.

I told her why I had come, but she cared more about my condition. She brought warm water and washed my feet. Only then did I notice the blisters pooled with blood. She massaged my legs and feet with butter, the most precious item in her home. That sacrifice touched me deeply. For the first time in days, I felt relief, safety, and a sense of home.

Once I rested, I wanted to know what had happened in Debre Markos. Had I panicked by leaving, or had I made the right decision? I sent a letter to a friend, asking him to respond through the same messenger, since we had no other way of communicating. His reply was grim: it was a scary situation, and I should either go far away or return and face it. The authorities were still trying to identify people. Eshetu Alemu's threats of raids that very night had been only a bluff.

After ten days, I decided to return to Debre Markos. I made the trip in one day, without stopping, so no one would know my route. I avoided Mengesha's house, returned home, and changed back into my normal attire. In Deboza, I had shaved my hair shorter, but not drastically different.

I visited my friends who were being held in a military camp. They assumed things would be fine, that the government would give "orientation" and then release everyone back to their families. Few realized the darkest days were still to come.

Having walked barefoot to Deboza and recovered in only a few days, I felt more confident. Part of me thought there might still be time; another part knew this was my chance to prepare and to be gone for good.

I stayed for twenty more days. On the last day, I received three clear warnings. The first came from two boys on the street, who mumbled, "What is he still doing here?" I understood. The second came from a close friend who told me she would rather not see me again. That was her way of urging me to leave. The third was from another friend in custody. Hidden in a small piece of paper under a dish cover, the note read: "Zinah needs to save himself." It was the clearest and most ominous warning yet. Either he had been tortured or knew torture was coming and that they were targeting me next. Arrests were typically carried out in the evenings or mornings, when people were expected to be at home.

Decision made.

I decided not to sleep at home. I knew they were coming for me, and in my absence, they would question my sister. I gave her a false lead, telling her I'd be hiding under a table at the high school. With over a hundred classrooms and dozens of tables in each, I hoped that if they fell for the story, it would waste precious time. I went to my mother's house instead. Even my sister didn't expect me to hide there.

Late in the morning, I cautiously returned home. Several feet away, I saw my younger brother waving me away. Suspicious, I paused until he came closer. Whispering, he told me armed men in a Land Rover had arrived, pointing guns at everyone and searching every room in my aunt's house. When they couldn't find me, they forced my sister to lead them to a friend's home. I rushed back to my mother's house and asked my aunt to buy me two pairs of shorts and sandals made from recycled tires.

I was ready to say goodbye to my friend, but he refused. Afraid that his association with me put him at risk, he insisted on coming along. Together, taking the least-used paths, we slipped out of town. With the sandals and my experience traveling to Deboza, I walked with confidence. I felt like a hero for escaping. I remained committed to my principles. I did not crumble under pressure. I was afraid of what would happen to me if I was caught, but I was not afraid of what would happen to me by trying to flee to safety. I constantly weighed the balance between the two evils. In my upbringing and a few books, I had read, and from stories I had heard, it was clear to me: there would be some struggle and some suffering while standing up for things I believed in. I dodged the bullet.

My friend was my age, in the same grade, but he constantly admired me, which boosted my ego. That day, we made it to Deboza, back to the house where I had stayed before. We received a warm welcome, spent the night, and resumed our journey even farther than I had gone on my first trip. This time, there was no hesitation. My fate was sealed; I had to keep moving forward.

I wore these kinds of sandals that were made of recycled tires

I had traveled this far, nor heard anyone who had. But I remembered some family routes: Markos to Yeboqla, Yeboqla to Kuyi, Kuyi to Bichena, and from Bichena to Yeduha, then to Gebsit. Gebsit, my destination, was where my father, uncles, and grandfather all had roots.

The route I traversed in the one year I spent hiding in the countryside.

We left Kuyi and reached Bichena, resting at my uncle Aya Imru Abebe's house. That night was full of encouragement and support. In the morning, he pointed us in the right direction. At one point, my friend collapsed in exhaustion. I worried I had made a mistake bringing him, but after resting, he recovered, and we pressed on.

We passed through the town where I had once attended elementary school and finally arrived in Gebsit. My beloved uncle, Ayaya Zewude, my father's older brother, welcomed us. He was a hardworking, serious, respected man.

Gebsit was my only hope to survive the dark days. This was the land of my father, my uncles, and my grandfather. During the Italian occupation, my grandfather had been a young patriot who fought from this very place. Here, family roots run deep.

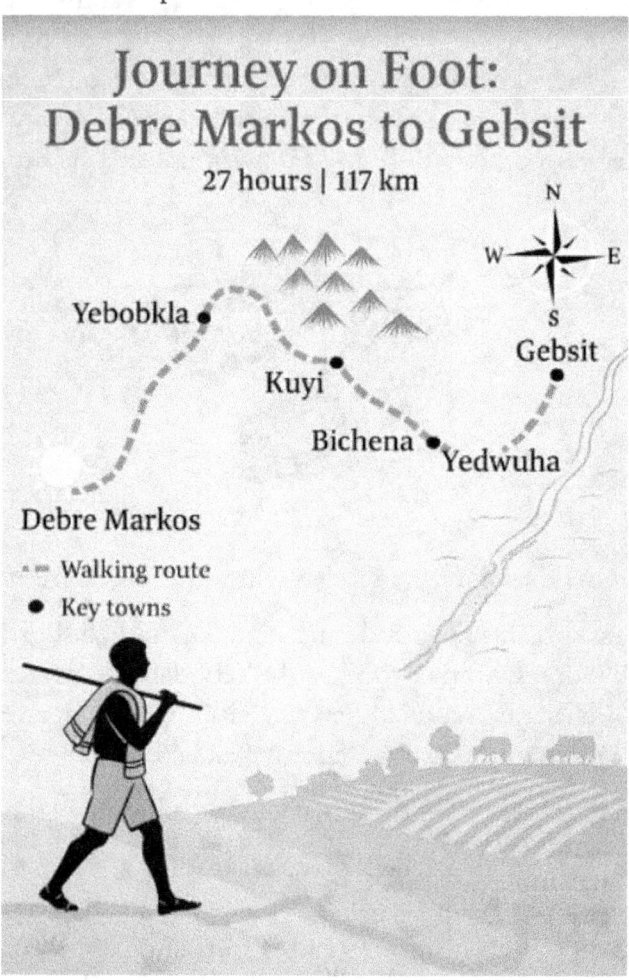

Journey on Foot: Debre Markos to Gebsit
27 hours | 117 km

Yebobkla
Kuyi
Gebsit
Bichena
Yedwuha
Debre Markos
- = Walking route
• Key towns

From Debre Markos to Kyui it took me most of the day, but I rested for the night. The following day I passed through Bichena, Yeduha and made it to Gebsit on the second day. I made this trip three times.

Here, I could survive, and I began to contemplate my long-term future. A new life had begun.

From Village to Village

I had no plans but only the hope of surviving one more day. We ate what was provided, assisted with farm work, and slept on the floor of an old, grass-thatched house. My friend Zeleke often complained of missing his mother. He scratched at his skin constantly, and his restlessness grew worse by the day. The excitement of evading the authorities, which once felt adventurous, had faded for him.

One evening, my uncle Ayaya spoke frankly with me.

"You are family," he said. "You are welcome here anytime. But I don't think your friend should stay."

He was right. I realized that if anything went wrong, it would likely be because someone became the weak link. A month after our arrival, Zeleke's daily complaints convinced me it was time for him to return home. I told him I had chosen this life, but it wasn't necessary for him to stay with me, and no one was looking for him, and we decided I needed to take him back. I explained to Ayaya that I would be back, then began the two-day trek to Markos with Zeleke. It took me four days for a round-trip walk.

On the first day, we walked from Gebsit to Kuyi, and the next day we reached Markos. At the edge of the city, I stayed with a trusted friend, keeping a low profile. Through him, I reconnected with my brother, my sister, and a few friends. This was my final goodbye. For the night, I stayed at Zeleke's family home. I rose before dawn to leave, but he woke and asked if I was heading back to Gebsit. To protect my path, I lied, telling him I was going toward Mota. In truth, I was bound for Gebsit again. After another two-day trek, I returned to Ayaya.

Once back, Ayaya and I discussed whether I should remain in Gebsit. He had another idea: moving me to Selelkula, a small village in the lowlands. It was a secure place, surrounded by cliffs with only two narrow footpaths leading in. From there, you could see anyone approaching from a distance. The family I stayed with kept alert dogs and lived in the shadow of a blood feud, which meant strangers approached with caution.

In Selelkula, I lived with Aya Asmamaw and Ignagn. Each day we worked on the farm. When Aya plowed with his oxen, I stood watch with his rifle. When I plowed, he took the rifle and guarded me. In the evenings, we returned home, shared dinner, and drank tela (homemade beer) or krari (an older, diluted version).

They often asked me about city life and whether people looked down on villagers as backward for lacking modern conveniences. I reassured them:

"The reason I am here, suffering as you do, is so one day there will be no haves and have-nots. Civilization must be shared by all."

Still, I knew staying too long in one place was risky. What they offered in food and shelter, I repaid in labor, but I didn't want to become a burden.

While in Selelkula, I learned that a classmate was nearby. We arranged to meet. Cautiously, I positioned myself on a wooded hill and watched him approach, making sure he was alone. Once we were close, I revealed myself, and we spoke of our hopes and options. He suggested Addis Ababa; I agreed it was possible, but for me, not yet. Afterward, I let him climb back up the hill before I returned to my hosts. I didn't want him to know exactly where I lived. It was time to move again.

The next stop was Abasilma, where Ayaya's in-laws lived. My uncle Ayaya Zewude, his older brother Ayawa Fenta, and Aya Asmamaw all had married sisters: Itete Tobiyaw, Itete Taitu, and Ignagn, respectively. Their father, Fitawurari Abebe Belew, had been a friend of my grandfather, Fitawurari Kebede Zeleke. From Selelkula, the trail to Abasilma wound downhill toward the Abay Gorge.

Abasilma's houses are perched on a hill, enclosed in a large compound. There were three traditional thatched huts and one house with a corrugated metal roof. The family kept many cattle and goats, so milk and butter were plentiful. The women's dresses were darkened at the neck, where they often rubbed butter into their hair.

In these homes, like the one in Gebsit and Selelkula, there were no chairs or tables. We sat on a medeb, a raised mud-and-stone platform sealed with cow dung. By day, it was for sitting by night, it became a bed covered with cowhide or goatskin. Our gabi served as both clothing and a blanket. Behind the houses, corn, potatoes, herbs, and grain storage bins lined the yard. Beehives dotted the compound. Truly, the land flowed with milk and honey.

At night, I slept in different places: sometimes under the eaves on a loft outside, beside a beehive I planned to kick if enemies came. Sometimes, in the open, surrounded by cattle that served as both guard and alarm; sometimes in the cornfield, where the dry leaves rustled at the slightest movement, though sometimes it was only the wind that startled me.

In the foreground from left to right, Zeleke, Mekdes, Yohanes, and Mesfin. In the background, Wubetu, Sefrash, and Yewul.

51

When my father sat in prison, surrounded by walls that muffled questions he dared not ask. To inquire about me openly would have been dangerous. Yet he searched for answers in silence. He requested something simple, something no guard would suspect. He asked for photographs of all the children.

When the pictures were finally placed in his hands, he looked, and then he stopped. Mine was missing.

The absence spoke louder than words. I was not in prison. I was not in the photograph. Somewhere out there, I was still alive, hidden and beyond their grasp. In that instant, father and son were bound by an unspoken understanding, a secret message passed through the void of a missing face.

Through it all, Ayaya guided and protected me, taking responsibility for my safety. Eventually, we decided I should move again, this time to Gubaya, near Yetmen.

By now, I have been hardened. I had long abandoned sandals, walking barefoot everywhere. My hands and legs were scratched and scarred from farm work, yet I labored like any seasoned farmer. The family I joined in Gubaya felt cold and distant, strangers who barely knew my kin. Perhaps they were too poor to host me fully, but I contributed my share of labor, hoping to ease their burden.

Still, a question haunted me: Was this my cause? To wander from farm to farm, working fields, waiting for fate? I had no money, no resources, no plans, but I knew my destiny was mine to claim.

Then a messenger arrived, summoning me to Yetmen. I had nothing to pack, just grab my stick and my gabi, and I was ready to go anywhere. When I arrived, Ayaya was waiting. He told me my mother had come searching for me. She was waiting in Dejen.

My heart swelled with pride. She had traveled far with only rumors as guidance. Even if she suspected I was in Gebsit, Selelkula, Abasilma, or Gubaya, how could she know which farm, which hut, which laborer I had become? She only knew that I might have gone to my father's homeland,

and that only my uncles might know. She was wise enough to follow the faintest trail, and that wisdom far outmatched the eagerness of my enemies who wanted to capture me.

We walked 19 kilometers from Yetmen to Dejen along the side of the paved road, arriving in about three hours. In town, I was shocked to see Asru (Aya Muluken's girlfriend) and her friend Mulunesh, both teachers from Robu Gebeya. They were more than friends. I had memorable times with them. It was hard not to greet them. They passed within feet of us, but Ayaya urged me to stay silent. He was right. Speaking to them would have risked everything.

We found my mother sitting on the porch of a hotel, scanning each passerby. When she saw me, disguised as a farmer, she contained her emotions, careful not to draw attention.

Before it was too late, Ayaya had to leave. He handed me a travel pass, written in his name as Zewde Kebede, but with a small error which read "Zewdu." From that day forward, I carried that name.

Ayaya had fulfilled his mission: he had protected me and now handed me safely to my mother. Together, we prepared to journey to Addis Ababa.

Reflection

Looking back, I see that my journey through Gebsit, Selelkula, Abasilma, and Gubaya was not just about survival. It was about transformation. Each village hardened me, stripped away comfort, and forced me to live as the people lived. I became a farmer, guard, wanderer, and fugitive all at once. What I lacked in resources, I learned to replace with resilience.

Yet beneath the hardship, there was always the thread of family and my uncles who sheltered me, my mother who searched with unshakable determination. My survival was not my own doing. It was carried by the loyalty and wisdom of those who believed in me. When my mother's eyes met mine in Dejen, I understood something significant: no matter how far

I wandered, no matter how invisible I tried to make myself, I was never truly lost.

Through the Lion's Gate

The hotel lobby was crowded. My mother had been there for over a day, speaking quietly over coffee, exchanging smiles with strangers. I stayed in the shadows, a silent observer. Every face could be a threat. Every glance is a potential exposure.

We passed Asru and Mulunesh. We haven't seen each other in a long time. It might unsettle them to see me in that condition. It is not good for them. Someone might see us talk to each other. Who else could be around? I didn't know. Danger moved in every corner, silent and unpredictable. My mother could not afford a mistake. Neither could I.

Questions came that were innocent and casual, but I answered slowly and deliberately, as if I were confused. Words stumbled from my lips. Gibberish. I wanted them to see a simple village boy, clueless, out of place, unaware of the world around him.

My mother laughed, both nervous and happy, that we were reunited. For over a year, I worked hard to assimilate with the farmers. It would be tough for anyone to think this was a 12th-grade student wearing a Roamer watch on his wrist and Levi jeans with leather shoes to go with it. Here, barefoot with cracked skin on my feet and ashy legs with wounds and scratches. I also spoke with a farmer's accent, and it made my mother laugh, and when people ask, she would say, "He is just silly,". Smoothly, convincingly. When asked who I was, she invented a story: a child born to a farmer, abandoned years ago, now reclaimed to live in the city. The lie flowed naturally, shielded us both.

I was invited to drink a bottle of Coke. I pretended I had never seen anything like it. I looked towards my mother as if I was asking if it was okay to drink it. I was drinking in a very awkward way, placing the neck of the bottle in my mouth rather than sipping it. Laughter rippled through the crowd. I smiled, embarrassed, but inside, I grinned. The act was working.

I kept my head low. I avoided eye contact with anyone. Every movement is calculated. Every gesture is part of the act. At dawn, the real journey would begin with the road, the danger, the unknown.

On the main road in front of the hotel, my cousin Ato Belay waited in a Soviet-made truck, engine idling, dust swirling around the tires. My mother spoke with him, and soon it was decided: I would ride along. We made a pact that if I was recognized, I would fend for myself. My mother would deny knowing me, and my cousin would treat me as nothing more than another passenger.

The road from Dejen plunged steeply, snaking through the Blue Nile canyon. The view was breathtaking, but I perched precariously atop a fully loaded truck, no seatbelt, no place to lie down, nothing to hold me steady. Each bump on the unpaved road jolted my body, and more than once I feared being thrown off.

Crossing the Blue Nile bridge ended the descent, but a long climb began. Uphill, endlessly uphill. Hours dragged, the truck groaning under its weight, the air thinner with each bend. The road felt eternal. Still, I reminded myself: this was a small price for the life ahead. Addis Abeba, a modern city, far removed from the rough year I had survived.

The true test awaited at Entoto. A police checkpoint, a place where discovery meant everything, could end. I prepared carefully. I picked at old farm wounds on my legs until they bled. I had not brushed my hair or teeth for days. As the truck slowed, I curled into myself, resting my head on my knees, squinting as though my vision had failed. Flies swarmed my legs, buzzing without mercy.

A soldier approached. He demanded my identification. I raised my head only slightly, blinking in confusion, pretending not to understand. My appearance, dirty, unkempt, and with wound scabs, made him recoil. I fumbled deliberately, clumsy and slow. Suspicion flickered across his eyes, then he was disgusted. With a flick of his hand, he waved me off, muttering that the travel pass did not matter.

Relief washed over me. I had crossed safely, slipping unnoticed through the lion's gate. But as the truck rumbled on and the checkpoint disappeared behind us, triumph was absent. Deep in my chest, I carried a weight of hope and fear.

Friends. Survivors. Hiding in plain sight under the nose of a brutal military dictatorship had kept me alive, but nearly all my schoolmates, teachers, and even the principal had been executed. The emptiness pressed down. I contemplated striking at the enemy in the capital itself. Perhaps naive, perhaps foolish, but it felt like it was possible. A dagger to the heart of the oppressor.

Ahead, Addis Abeba loomed. Sharper teeth, quieter traps. The lion's den was not behind me; it had only just begun.

The Price of Shelter

The last time I had been in Addis Abeba was when we moved from Asela back to Gojjam. Now, returning as a young man on the run, I felt like a stranger. The city seemed larger, louder, and sharper than I remembered, an endless maze of streets where danger might be hiding at every corner.

I tried to keep my head down, but one thing betrayed me: I was still barefoot. The hot asphalt burned my feet, each step reminding me how much I stood out. In Addis, even the poor wore shoes. Walking barefoot marked me as a farm boy out of place, exposed, and vulnerable. My first disguise would have to be simple: I needed shoes.

We checked into a modest hotel near Merkato, the sprawling marketplace at the city's heart. My mother, ever resourceful, wasted no time. She had been married more than once, run a hotel in Hamusit, and learned the art of survival. She knew how to call in favors, and with a few quick phone calls, she began arranging meetings. Her goal was clear: buy me enough time to disappear into the city until I could stand on my own.

The first man we visited was an old acquaintance of my parents from their days in Debre Markos. He once lived with them while attending high school, later joining the Air Force as an aircraft mechanic. Now he worked for Ethiopian Airlines, a prestigious post in a country where even owning a mule gave a man status. He even owned a car, a luxury reserved for the elite.

We waited a long time for him, and when he finally arrived, it was as though he had forgotten us. His words were distant, cautious, measured. He knew, or at least suspected, the danger I was in. Helping me could cost him his job, his freedom, perhaps even his life. I could see the calculations in his eyes: gratitude for my parents' past kindness weighed against the risk of being exposed. The answer was clear. We left empty-handed, disappointed but not surprised.

The next day, we tried again. This time, we visited a cousin who lived in Addis. Late in the evening, he turned on the television. The last time I saw one was in Asmara, when I was thirteen. On the screen, the Red Army was fighting the Nazis. I had heard about the war on the radio, but watching it play out in motion, with sound, fascinated me.

My cousin, however, was less enthusiastic. He had risen from a humble beginning to become the owner of five trucks, one of the wealthiest men in our extended family. To him, socialism was a threat, not a promise. He did not like me watching the program. With a sharp look, he turned off the TV and left the room. I had hoped he might hire me as an assistant to one of his drivers. I dreamed of hiding among the cargo, slipping onto a ship, and leaving the country altogether. But when we explained my situation, he too recoiled. The risk was too great. Another door closed.

Through it all, I stayed in the background. I followed my mother as if I were her servant, never her son. It was safer that way. To strangers, I was just a quiet boy carrying her bag. In reality, I was always ready to run. The streets of Addis were my new jungle, full of cover but also of predators.

One afternoon in Merkato, a young man from Hamusit recognized me. He remembered me as the energetic boy who used to visit from Gojjam. Now he saw only a subdued, timid figure. My mother, quick as always, told him I had dropped out of school and become a farmer, and that she was trying to help me start over. He believed her and even pitied me. I was glad he asked no further questions. My disguise had worked.

Finally, we turned to someone my mother trusted more deeply, which was her former sister-in-law. Though divorced from her brother, she remained on cordial terms. This time, fortune turned in our favor. Adjusting her story to minimize risk, my mother asked only for a place where I could rest my head. Nothing more.

That same day, another relative was staying in the house, Melaku, a soldier recovering from wounds sustained in the Ethio-Somali war. He was active, despite his injury, and insisted I should not rely solely on the temporary travel pass. If soldiers stopped me again, they would wonder why I had not returned home. With his help, I applied for a Kebele ID.

At the office, I stayed in character. When asked to sign, I claimed I could not write, and they gave me an ink pad for my thumbprint. When I was told to relax for the photo, I pretended not to understand. They were convinced I was exactly what I wanted them to believe, an uneducated farm boy.

With my new ID, I had a legal place in the city. My aunt offered me a small, long-closed room with a window, a door, and a bed that filled nearly all the space. There were only two feet left to stand, but to me, it was a refuge.

It was not without its costs. That first night, I discovered bedbugs. They started small, but as the days passed, they grew fat on my blood. Each bite was a reminder of my predicament. Yet I accepted it. It is better to lose a little blood to insects than to soldiers or executioners. My choices were clear, and I had no complaints, only gratitude that I had survived another day.

With shelter secured, my mother and I allowed ourselves one small reprieve. We went to Filwuha, the hot spring bathhouse. I remember the feeling of the mineral water washing away the dirt, the dust, and the fear. The last time I bathed was in a seasonal creek near Gebsit. This was different. It felt like a baptism, a momentary cleansing, a fragile reminder that life still offered beginnings, even in the midst of danger.

58

Addis Abeba had not given me comfort, but it had given me shelter. For now, that was enough.

The city was a jungle, its concrete and asphalt teeming with predators both seen and unseen. Every friendly face could be a threat, every conversation a trap. Yet in this jungle, I was learning to move like a shadow, to breathe in silence, to survive. The lion's den had changed and so had I. But my fight was far from over.

A Dangerous Ride

I now had an ID, a place to stay, and a small amount of money. My mother and I discussed what I should do next. One of her ideas was for me to get a driver's license. She said I could work as a chauffeur, and since I was not yet settled anywhere, it might even be safer to always be on the move. I liked the thought, but I didn't think I had the time or money for training. Ever resourceful, my mother suggested we could bribe someone to get me the license. Even at nineteen, I stood firm.

"I don't support corruption," I told her. "And I don't want anything I don't earn."

She wasn't happy with my answer, but she respected it. She wished me good luck and went back home, leaving me to fend for myself.

It didn't take long before I found labor work in Gofa, where a new garage was under construction. They hired me to dig the mechanical pit, a backbreaking job, but I welcomed the hard labor. It kept me fit, and I hoped that in time they might take me on as a trainee to repair cars. Some days I was asked to clean engine parts. I left the house early in the morning and returned late at night, keeping my distance from the family that sheltered me in Lideta. The less they knew about my life, the better.

From the little money I made, I went to Asmara Road to learn how to drive. Driver training was in a Fiat 600. I also learned how to ride motorcycles. I was thinking that instead of fighting in some remote place, the possibility of fighting in the capital city was possible. I also wanted to be familiar with the city street by street. I could take a taxi or the bus, but sometimes I walked from Lideta to Janmeda, and that was about two hours.

One afternoon, after work, I boarded a crowded bus in Gofa heading to Lideta. As I was about to climb on, a tall man in a leather jacket shoved me hard aside and stepped in front of me. I wasn't sure if it was an accident or a deliberate show of disrespect, but my instincts told me to stay alert.

Inside, I stood next to a farmer carrying a stick, clearly fresh from Kera, where cattle were bought and slaughtered. The tall man positioned himself close to the farmer, one hand gripping the rail above, the other slipping into the farmer's pocket. He was a pickpocket. From his neat clothing and intimidating height, no one would suspect him of being a thief. The farmer, sensing what was happening, trembled but froze in fear, too intimidated to act.

I watched, waiting to see if the thief would produce something. His hand came out empty, but I was already angry. First, he had disrespected me. Now he had tried to rob a hardworking farmer. To me, both were offenses against the dignity of working people. My time in Berenta had made me one of them, and I couldn't stay silent.

I raised my voice so the thief could hear but spoke to the farmer.

"Why do you let him go in your pocket? What's the use of that stick if you won't defend yourself?"

The thief turned to me, his face twisting in anger. "F*** you!" he spat.

I didn't trade insults. Instead, I stepped forward and punched him square in the face. He went down hard, crashing into the crowd. He scrambled back up, wiping his face to check for blood.

"Do you want another punch?" I asked.

He pointed at the farmer. "Did I take anything? Did I? Did I?"

The farmer, emboldened, lifted his stick and smacked the thief on the hand. I laughed.

"There you go! Now you're using that stick for what it was meant for. Hit him again if you want to."

The thief's tone shifted. "I'll get you," he said darkly.

"I'm right here," I shot back. "Try me."

The farmer and I stood tall, side by side. The thief looked around, as if searching for help, but kept quiet, his earlier swagger gone. For a few minutes, we bragged loudly about how we stood up to him, but then the bus fell silent.

A man I knew from the garage leaned close and whispered, "You've made a big mistake."

I frowned. "How? By standing up to a thief?"

He shook his head. "That man isn't alone. They travel in groups of seven or eight at a time. You can't tell who they are, but they carry knives. Today could be the day they stab you. I hope you survive."

Fear surged through me. I scanned the crowded bus, trying to guess which passengers might be with him. Was this how I would die, stabbed on a bus, or bleeding out on the way to a hospital after surviving so much already?

When the bus reached my stop in Lideta, I knew they would also get off. I pushed my way to the front and leapt out as soon as the doors opened. Grabbing a heavy rock from the roadside, I turned and shouted, "No one gets off this bus! Whoever steps down first, I'll smash in the head."

The passengers froze. The driver yelled for those meant to get off, but they explained they were being threatened. Whenever someone twitched, I raised the rock, my eyes locked on them. No one dared move. Finally, frustrated and running late, the driver slammed the door shut and pulled away.

I didn't wait to see what happened next. As soon as the bus gathered speed, I sprinted down the streets, weaving through narrow alleys, making turn after turn until I reached home, breathless but alive.

Reflection

That night, as I lay on my bed, my heart still racing, I realized how thin the line was between courage and recklessness. I had stood up for dignity, both mine and the farmer's, but I had also placed myself in grave danger. The man on the bus was right, but I could have been stabbed. My life ended in an instant.

Still, I did not regret my actions. To me, silence in the face of disrespect or injustice felt like a slow death, a surrender of everything I had endured to survive. But I also began to see that survival required more than fists and defiance. It demanded strategy and knowing when to fight, when to step back, and when to disappear.

It was a lesson I would carry with me: that the struggle for dignity is never without risk, but wisdom lies in choosing battles carefully. On that bus in Addis Ababa, I had fought with my fists. In the future, I would need to fight with something more powerful.

The Price of Suspicion

I explored Addis Abeba as much as I could. One day, I was in Merkato and passed a fancy, well-lit store selling suits. There, I spotted my friend Belachew, the one I had exchanged letters with when I was in Kuyi. I paused, careful not to call his name, hoping he would recognize me without speaking. He stepped out quietly. We exchanged greetings, and I asked a favor: to make a mental note of people he saw in the city so I could learn who were friends and who were foes. To my surprise, he told me one of my best friends, Bayush, was also in Addis. We arranged to meet, and she later invited me to a meal at her home, the best meal I had in a long time. We remained in touch for many years after.

One day, my father passed by the same store. Belachew stopped him and connected us. My father was pleased to see me in Addis, remarking that it was the perfect place to hide. "Living in Addis Abeba," he said, "is like being a pebble in the ocean." I believed him, and at least until Melaku began to notice me.

Over time, the way I dressed changed. Gone were the ragged clothes of the countryside. I now wear green trousers tucked into polished red military boots with side zippers, and a sharp jacket over my shoulders, and my father's gift, the Roamer watch, on my wrist. At a glance, I looked like a civilian officer. People gave me a wide berth, few daring to meet my eyes.

The Roamer watch my father had before I was born. He gave it to me when I was 16.

I even carried myself differently. In Berenta, Gojam I had been a barefoot farm boy; in Addis, I blended with the city. My high school friend

Sisay, also a relative, sometimes met me. Together, we spoke of dreams, imagining even forming a resistance movement, but those were whispers, fleeting and cautious.

One afternoon, I stood at a crowded bus stop. When the bus pulled up, I checked the number, recognized my route, and boarded. Ordinarily, I thought until I realized someone was watching.

Melaku.

He had been observing me for some time. Later, I overheard him speaking with Antye, a student living with the family next door:

"How does someone from the deep countryside," Melaku pressed, "move about the city within months with no trouble? Look at how he dresses. He travels freely, reads bus numbers, when he couldn't even sign his own name before, only a thumbprint for his ID."

I froze in the shadows, listening.

Antye replied, calm and protective: "That is the revolution at work. Farmers from backward villages transform into the proletariat. Zewudu is an example. With opportunity, many his age could do the same."

Melaku's voice hardened. "Too fast. I've seen others change, but not like this. He is not who he says he is."

The words chilled me. Melaku had been stalking me all along. His sharp eyes missed nothing: my clothes, my movements, even the way I boarded a bus. Loyal to the government, I knew he would turn me in once his suspicion solidified.

I reflected on how quickly a haven could become a trap. Addis Abeba had given me shelter, freedom, and a taste of city life, but beneath its surface, danger stayed. Every street could conceal enemies, every face, a threat. Survival now demanded more than hiding in plain sight; it required vigilance, calculation, and knowing whom to trust.

From that moment, each step I took in the city felt heavy with danger. My days in Addis were numbered. quietly, I went to the Kebele office, requesting a travel pass to visit my family for the New Year. They issued it without question. Without telling anyone, I bought my ticket, boarded a bus, and left the city behind.

As the bus rumbled northward toward Gojam, relief and dread mingled. Addis had offered a taste of freedom, yet it had also taught me a vital lesson: freedom never comes without cost. Appearances could protect, trust could deceive, and vigilance was life itself. Ahead lay Andabet, my destination, and with it, the next steps in a journey far from over.

Reflection:

In the quiet moments on the bus, I understood something essential about myself. Survival was not only about hiding or fighting, but it was also about adaptation, patience, and careful calculation. Courage was quiet, not loud or heroic. It came from knowing when to move, when to stand still, and when to trust instincts honed by a year of hardship. I had learned to read people, streets, and danger before it read me. Each challenge I faced, each risk I took, sharpened me into someone who could endure not merely by force, but by understanding the delicate balance between freedom and peril.

Part II: Survival

Chapter 4 - Another Direction Another Day

The bus rolled steadily along the same road that had carried me to Addis Abeba months before. This time, I was not perched precariously atop a fully loaded truck, but seated inside a bus, cushioned and safe. It felt like a small upgrade and a fleeting comfort, but I knew better than to relax completely. I could not know what lay ahead, and caution had become my second skin..

We passed through Dejen, the town where I first reunited with my mother. I remembered the tension, the fear of recognition, the way I had carefully avoided speaking to Asru and Mulunesh. Yet there were also relief and protection in that memory, a reminder that danger and shelter often walked side by side.

Then Yetmen, and I recalled the day I met Ayaya six months ago, the tentative friendship and cautious trust. Bichena followed, where I had spent time with Aya Imru during my first escape from Debre Markos. Each town marked a step in my journey, a memory of survival and connection, a chapter in a life constantly on the move, each stop adding something to my escape.

From Bichena to Mota, the landscape shifted. Rolling fields, scattered huts, grazing cattle, the countryside stretched in quiet beauty. It was New Year's Eve, and the familiar rhythm of rural life stirred something deep within me: nostalgia, warmth, and the echoes of Gebsit. Even those days of hardship were tinged with the care and protection of my relatives, the small acts of love that had shaped me.

My father's words came back to me, spoken often in Amharic: "አገር ቀሚስ ነው." The country is a dress. A dress covers, protects, gives dignity. It protects us from the elements, shelters us from exposure, and reminds us of who we are. That phrase had always resonated, and as the bus moved steadily through the countryside, it felt truer than ever. The land, in all its beauty and danger, was both my refuge and my teacher, a garment that is worn sometimes thin, sometimes warm.

I leaned back in my seat, taking it all in, the winding roads, the distant hills, the cooking smoke rising over the scattered settlements. Each mile carried me closer to Andabet, via Mota. The journey from Mota to Andabet would be on foot, something as daunting as it is inevitable. I was, however, getting closer to a future that I would shape with the lessons of the past. And yet, the road reminded me: survival is never easy, and the journey is never over.

Reflection:

As the bus hummed along, I realized that Andabet was more than a destination. It was a state of awareness, of understanding one's place in the world. Every hardship, every narrow escape, had taught me vigilance, patience, and the value of small, careful choices. The countryside, with its familiar rhythms and quiet beauty, reminded me that life offers both shelter and challenge in equal measure. I understood that the path ahead would demand courage and cunning, but also that I carried within me the tools to endure. The journey to Andabet was not just a bid for safety. It was also a preparation, a reminder that survival is a balance of strength, intelligence, and hope.

A New Beginning in Andabet

I arrived in Mota safely and went to a lady who sold Tej (mead). This was the same place my mother had stayed in when she came to Gojam, about twenty-one years earlier. I was now nineteen. They also had a room for rent, and I told the lady that I was a relative of my uncle, Aba Birru, so that she might cooperate with me and help me learn how to get to Andabet. She did not seem to believe me. She never smiled during our conversation and carried herself with a reserved, suspicious air. Still, I spent the night there, knowing that my journey would continue the next morning.

This time, unlike my mother, who once traveled away from here, I was going in the opposite direction. It was New Year's, and my plan was to cross the Blue Nile bridge, the only passage. The bridge was guarded, but I hoped fortune would allow me through without interrogation. It was a harder route to Andabet, with steep declines, long stretches of footpaths, and miles of uphill travel. The easier way would have been through Debre Markos, Bahir Dar, Hamusit, and Este, but that route was too risky for me.

I traveled with a couple of people for part of the way, but eventually, they turned toward their homes, leaving me alone. When I reached the bridge, luck was on my side and there were no guards. After crossing, I asked for a place to spend the night. Villagers directed me to a farmer's home where I could sleep for a dime. That evening, I sat with the family by the fireplace. They had not yet seen the new currency, so I showed them a twenty-five-cent coin, along with one- and five-birr notes. I kept the rest hidden, but the little I shared sparked conversation and trust. They welcomed me warmly, and in the morning, the farmer gave me fresh milk before I left.

As I was about to go, a man approached with a Lee Enfield rifle, striding quickly as if ready for confrontation. His posture alarmed me, but I steadied myself and walked toward him. I asked if he was supposed to be guarding the bridge, speaking with confidence and even a slight tone of demand. Caught off guard, he asked me, "Why?" I replied that I was surprised to find the bridge unguarded. He asked for my ID and travel pass, which I handed over without hesitation. The way I carried myself seemed to unsettle him.

I then asked him to point me in the right direction, and when he said he was going to a Peasant Association meeting, I insisted that I should come with him to pay homage to the chairman. He agreed, and because I entered with him, the others assumed we were together. The meeting was held in a house where people sat in a semicircle on a raised medeb. They were drinking tela, and a woman moved around filling glasses. I asked her to bring a kettle for the chairman, a gesture that earned me unexpected favor. When I rose to leave, the chairman asked me to sit again. He stood, thanked me for honoring him and the peasants, and gave me his blessing for the journey. One of his men stepped outside and pointed me in the right direction.

I told them I was heading to Este, farther than my true destination. If anyone followed, they would go past me and lose time searching. Survival required not only courage but also deception.

I walked for hours before reaching a small town. Unsure of where I was, I saw a man harvesting wheat with a sickle. As I approached, he suddenly ran toward me with the sickle raised. The memory of an earlier attempt on my life flashed through my mind, and I braced for another attack. But as he drew close, I realized it was my older brother. He was not running to harm me. He was running with joy. He embraced me warmly, and at last, I had arrived in Andabet.

The part of my life in Addis Abeba had closed, and a new chapter had begun. My troubles were not yet over, but for the first time in a long while, I was not alone.

Reflection

That reunion with my brother felt like stepping out of the shadows. I had crossed rivers and borders, deceived men with rifles, and earned the trust of strangers, but this moment reminded me that survival is about finding your people again. My father's words about "a country being like a dress" echoed in me. Home is not only the land we walk on; it is also the arms that welcome us, even when life has torn us apart. And yet, I knew my story was still unfolding. Safety was never permanent, and belongings always carried a cost.

Crossing into New Trials

I came to Andabet for two reasons. Addis Abeba was no longer safe for me, and I saw little opportunity to keep fighting the military junta from there. My friend had urged me to wait, to live quietly, hoping something might change. I told him I respected that, but for me, the only path was to seek those who had taken up arms. I had heard that the EPRA, the armed wing of the EPRP, was operating near Belesa and Ibnat. That was only a

70

day or two's walk away. But I knew: the closer I moved to the conflict zone, the higher the scrutiny, the higher the risks. I was walking into a warzone, where every step could mean a tighter noose or an unexpected ally.

My mother had learned I had left Addis and come to stay with my brother. She wrote him a letter, but not to me, and urging him to intervene. She wanted me to surrender, to stop living on the run. My brother, to my disbelief, not only agreed but went to the Peasant Association himself. He told them I was hiding in his house. He even declared that he opposed the government and wished to surrender as well. He asked the chairman to write him a letter to that effect. The lack of discussing his idea with me hurt me more than I could admit.

I could hardly believe it. After all my refusals to submit, after a year and a half of surviving in hiding, I had come to my brother for safety, but only to be exposed by him. He didn't seem to understand that more than 250 students and teachers had already been executed from my high school. I told him that what he did was a mistake. Decisions about my life are mine alone. Others might help, but no one else decides for me.

He grew angry, saying, "Who do you think you are? You're no better than the millions of progressive people."

"I don't compare myself to anyone," I told him. "But I decide what is best for me."

It was clear we would not change each other's minds. Still, since the chairman had kindly written letters for us, I asked my brother to take me to him so I could thank him. My intention was to get a letter pretending to thank the chairman. In private, I told the chairman that the letter in my name put me in danger. If a zealous cadre saw it, he might kill me outright and then claim he had only acted on discovering a fugitive. I suggested a safer alternative: a letter stating that Ato Imbiale Belew had volunteered to go to Setit Humera to join the government's "green campaign" to harvest crops. The name was false my way of quietly rebelling, declaring "tell him I refused" in hidden form. The chairman didn't question it. I gave him two Birr for his trouble, and he wrote the letter.

71

My brother never knew. Together, we traveled on to Este, then caught a pickup truck to Hamusit. From there, we entered my mother's house by the back gate. She was overjoyed, believing I had agreed at last to surrender. I found a bag of my clothes from Debre Markos in one room, but the underwear was missing. The sight chilled me. Whoever had taken it assumed I would never return, alive or dead. That small theft was a reminder: some people care less about your life than about what they can take from you. The loss of a personal item reminded me of the uncertainty that influenced my every decision.

My mother wanted to invite neighbors and family to celebrate. She told my sisters I had returned to live in peace. I told her no, I needed privacy. In the morning, we sat face-to-face. I expressed my disappointment about the plans they made without telling me. "If I surrender," I said, "I will be tortured and killed. The better option would be for me to take my own life and let you bury me. Otherwise, you must step back and let me follow my own path." The desperation in my voice matched the fear growing in my chest.

"Why are you so adamant?" she asked. "Is this some kind of religion you follow, that you show such absolute determination?"

To show her what I said, I lit a candle and held my surrender letter over the flame. As it caught fire, she cried, "Why? Why?"

"I want to fight or die with dignity," I told her. "Not beg for mercy from people I despise."

At that moment, my brother walked in, snatched the burning paper, stamped out the flame, and saw it was the letter he had arranged for me. I told him to stay out of my business. Then I changed my clothes, shifting from city style to farmer's dress to match the cover story in my new letter. My mother finally agreed: "Escort him up to Gonder. Then come back and let him pursue his goals." Even as I fought for my dignity, my mother's desire for my safety was palpable.

On the road, as we waited for a bus, my younger sisters ran up. They wanted to hug me goodbye. I pushed them back, saying, "This is the last time you will ever see me. Goodbye." Then I boarded the bus.

At the Woreta checkpoint, we passed without trouble. At Addis Zemen, I presented my pass, and again we passed. From the corner of my eye, I watched my brother's surprise at how smoothly I managed. I thought to myself: This is what it means to live as a master of disguise. My ability to stay hidden was becoming my biggest strength and an art.

We reached Gonder and walked the streets, looking for transport to Humera. In the distance, we saw my mother, unmistakable in her white dress, high heels, and umbrella. She insisted we sit down together. In a house where tela was served, she argued for mediation, for clemency. I kept my guard up. At one point, my brother stepped out, and I slipped outside by another door to make sure he wasn't betraying me. He wasn't. When he returned, I told them both it was time to part ways. I saw them board their bus, then hurried away to hide. Every step, every decision was a choice between trust and suspicion.

I spent the night locked in a small, rented room. In the morning, I searched for a truck heading west. At a gas station, I found one bound for Humera. The assistant quoted me ten Birr. I agreed, but his questions about money, about lodging, made me suspicious. Still, I followed him to his house for the night.

His mother interrogated me endlessly. I spun a farmer's tale: a stepmother interfering in my marriage, oxen dead, no future but Humera. She mocked me as a fool. Later, her son pointed to a spot on the floor where I was sleeping. I remembered the pickpocket in Addis and stayed alert. I kept a clay pot within reach as a weapon. My guard remained up, even in the place that made me feel safer.

Sure enough, in the night, he crept toward me. Before he could touch me, I leapt up, screaming, "In the name of the Holy Trinity!" and brandished the pot. He backed off quickly, muttering something about checking on chickens for the trip. I knew the truth: he had tried to rob me.

At dawn, we went to the truck. Before we left Gonder, soldiers stopped us at a checkpoint. Suddenly, about twenty men in full gear swarmed us, armed with AK-47s, grenades, the works. My heart pounded. I thought my brother's warning was about to come true and that I would be dragged off the truck and shot.

But instead, they climbed aboard, relaxed and cheerful. "ኩራ እንደ ካራማራ!" they shouted. Be proud like Karamara! They were government escorts, protecting the convoy from ambushes. Ironically, I had hoped for just such an ambush so I could slip away to join the rebels. Still, I smiled, ate their rations, even held a rifle for one of them, pretending to fear that I would lower their guard.

After three long days, we reached Humera. One chapter of my life had closed. But I knew: my troubles were far from over.

Reflection

Each step of the journey carried new dangers, grave misunderstandings from within my family, deception from strangers, checkpoints, and armed soldiers. Yet through it all, one truth became clear: survival required not just courage, but constant vigilance, cunning, and an unshakable commitment to my own path. Even when those closest to me tried to steer me another way, I had to trust my convictions. I was walking deeper into uncertainty, but also closer to the struggle I had chosen.

The Final Frontier

I had arrived at the outskirts of Humera. I asked the truck driver to stop and climbed down, saying goodbye to the soldiers, the assistant, and the two women who had shared the road with me. A new episode was about to begin at the very edge of Ethiopia, the final frontier. The dusty air, the barren land, everything felt like a new chapter and that my feet finally marked a new beginning.

I crossed the street and walked toward the entrance of the volunteer crop-harvesters' camp. At the gate, a man with no firearms leaned against a wall. I greeted him and explained that I had come on my own to join the Green Campaign, the Derg's massive state-driven farming effort. I expected a welcome, perhaps a simple, "We are glad you came." Instead, his words were sharp and suspicious.

"We were forced here," he said bitterly. "Some are sick. No one comes here willingly. You must have burned a house or killed someone. There is no way you came here innocently. You must be examined."

He summoned armed men in uniform, six in total, and he told them I was suspicious. They did not seem as agitated as he was. My heart raced, afraid they might search my pockets and find the Roamer watch in my pocket, a sign of who I really was. But instead, they dismissed him and asked if I was hungry. They gave me thin porridge, which I ate quietly, my mind turning over possible dangers. The watch, the last remnant of my old life, seemed to weigh heavily on me now.

I studied each of them, how they sat, where they rested their rifles. If they tried to harm me, I was ready to seize a weapon, as I had once imagined on my last day at high school. I had trained myself for moments like this when the difference between life and death came down to seconds and decisions.

That night, one of them said, "Have him sleep in the middle." My body tensed. That was a red flag. They wanted me where I could not escape.

I did not sleep well. The porridge unsettled my stomach, and I lay restless, listening. Before dawn, I sat up and said I needed to go and relieve myself. One of them told a guard to follow me with his rifle. Another red flag. There were no latrines. Relief was taken in the open fields, now dry and dusty after the harvest.

I calculated my move. I positioned myself against the slight wind so that the guard would be forced to turn away from the smell. Fortune was with me. I had diarrhea, and the sound of my struggle made him avert his eyes. It was a strange sort of luck, by luck nonetheless. When I finished, I slipped quietly away, crossed the road, and ran under the cover of a truck's dust cloud until I reached Humera city.

In town, I hid for hours in a tea house, sipping slowly, watching the street to be sure no one followed. Later, under the shade of a tree, I wondered what my next step would be. That is when a man named Beyene approached me.

"Do you need work?" he asked.

"Yes," I answered.

He offered me thirty birr a month and brought me to his house. His wife gave me food, and my sleeping spot was inside their fenced compound. Like in Addis Ababa, I left early each morning and returned before dark, sometimes hauling water by donkey. I discovered later they had searched my pockets while I slept. His wife told me they had only taken my money to "keep it safe," but I felt exposed and powerless.

Still, this was a temporary shelter, a place to plan my escape to join the rebels nearby or to reach Sudan.

Beyene owned a large sorghum farm and a camel. He asked me to cut and pile the dry stalks. I worked hard, and one day he beamed with pride. "You've done beyond what I expected," he said.

He told me his story: how he had arrived in Humera from Tigray with nothing but a bed sheet around his neck and had built a life. He wanted me to see him as a role model, planting the seed that I, too, could become like him. But my dream was different, and my nightmare was still pressing.

He gave me an affectionate nickname: "Imbye." He often said, "Imbye, you are not a farmer. You are too fast, too smart. The way you handled the camel, jumping on it and riding it, shows you are more than this." I deflected, insisting I was just eager to learn. But he was not convinced. His praise made me uneasy. I knew I could see through the façade I had constructed for survival.

All the while, I gathered quiet knowledge. I saw the military trenches where EDU and the Derg had clashed. I tested paths toward Sudan, pretending to be lost. Villagers laughed at my "ignorance," pointing out Sudanese roads, a flagpole across the border, and the direction of the river.

Each careless answer they gave confirmed what I needed.

At the tailor's shop one day, I overheard rumors that Beyene had told people I would one day run an oil business with him and marry his daughter. That was a red flag. He had his plans for me, but they were not mine. I knew I had to leave.

To cross into Sudan, I had to face the Tekeze River, which had deep, swift spots and was crawling with crocodiles. I heard stories of people snatched while bathing or drowned trying to cross. But I also learned from traders, men from Chad, called Tikurir, that dusk and dawn were the usual crossing times. I would do the opposite.

My plan was to cross at high noon, when no one expected it, when both armies relaxed their guard. I would carry an axe to explain myself if stopped, claiming I was gathering firewood. I would take a wide arc south, then west, then north, keeping low in tall grass, using dry streambeds as cover.

Once, I crawled away silently from a tall Beni-Amir man carrying a dagger. Another time, a man shouted at me to stop, but I ignored him and pressed forward. Finally, I reached the riverbank.

The Tekeze lay before me, the last barrier. I studied the water, searching for a shallow point where the current slowed. I rolled my pants to keep them dry, then stepped in. The water reached my hips. I pushed forward, mindful of crocodiles, bracing against the current. On the opposite bank, three people were scooping water. They watched silently as I crossed.

At last, I stumbled onto the far side. My chest heaved with relief. I asked the people where to find the military to surrender and seek asylum.

I was out of Ethiopia. I had crossed into Sudan.

Reflection

Crossing the Tekeze was like stepping out of one life and into another. Each suspicion, each red flag, each small deception had brought me to this point. I had survived by learning to read danger, to listen more than I spoke, to move when the moment was right.

Humera had tested me: the false safety of Beyene's home, the lure of staying hidden, the pull of ordinary work. But my path was never ordinary. I was not meant to harvest sorghum or ride camels. My destiny lay beyond borders, beyond the reach of those who sought to capture me. My journey to Sudan was a deliberate decision to defy a life built on fear and escape into a world of freedom.

When I reached the far bank of the Tekeze, I felt both lighter and heavier free of Ethiopia, yet burdened with exile. I carried no belongings, no money, only my will to survive. But in that moment, I knew: the river had not only divided nations, it had also divided my life into before and after. The river, wide and unforgiving, reflected the divide between who I was and who I would become.

Chapter 5 - Crossing into the Unknown

The town I arrived in was Hamdayt, just across the Sudanese border. Arabic was the language spoken, but I knew none of it. Still, I asked if they could direct me to the Sudanese army stationed nearby, hoping to request asylum. I hesitated, knowing that every word spoken was another chance to be caught in someone else's narrative.

The soldiers eyed me with suspicion. They seemed accustomed to desperate men crossing over, but my sudden appearance puzzled them. "Maybe you were dropped off by the Ethiopians," one muttered. "Maybe you're a spy." They studied my empty hands, my bare pockets. Clearly, I carried nothing, yet they didn't want me lingering at the border. "Better if you move further into Sudan," they told me. Their words felt like an invitation, wrapped in the form of a warning.

That suited me just fine. I still feared being dragged back across the border. But I admitted I had no money and no idea where to go. They waved me off, and I walked to a small shack that served as a tea house. With the little money I had left, I bought tea and bread.

There, I met Woldai, a man who reminded me of Ato Beyene in Humera. Thin, sickly, with sharp eyes, he said he needed help with his work. He owned two donkeys and fetched water from the Tekeze River to sell in Hamdayt. If I worked for him, he promised meals and half the earnings. But he insisted he would "hold" my money for me. There it was again. Another offer with uncertainty. Another chance to put my trust in the hands of someone who might betray it.

I agreed, but I did not trust him. By now, I had learned: no matter where you are, Ethiopia or Sudan, trust could be a dangerous luxury.

Each day, I carried water from the Tekeze up into town, the townspeople calling after me "በእል ማይ" ("the one with water"), and I answered back. On the way back downhill, I rode the donkey. The animals looked strong at first, but the endless loads broke them down. Their exhaustion reflected my own, and I began to pity them.

At night, I handed the money to Woldie's wife. She told me they were "keeping it safe." I swallowed my anger, remembering what had happened with Ato Beyene. Meanwhile, I kept my distance from everyone, sometimes singing TPLF or ELF songs loudly enough for passersby to hear but never stopping to talk. They would shout encouragement, "ኣጆኻ ኣታ ሃወይ!" ("Courage, brother!"). However, I never revealed more of myself. In Hamdayt, survival meant being visible but unknowable. The songs were a subtle form of rebellion. It was a way to mark my place in a world where visibility was both necessary and dangerous.

After some time, I told Woldie I was ready to move deeper into Sudan. I asked for my share of the earnings. He refused. Another thief, I thought, another man who wanted to hold me by taking what I had earned. This time, I was not afraid. Here, I was not under Ethiopian terror. We were both refugees. I went to the local authorities and told them that I wanted to leave Hamdayt for Gedarif, a larger city, but Woldie was holding my money. Everyone in town knew I had worked honestly, day after day.

The officials summoned him and ordered him to pay me. Reluctantly, he handed me the money. I left Hamdayt immediately, boarding a truck for Gedarif.

In Gedarif, I stood lost by the roadside, unsure where to go. Fortune intervened. I spotted a man dressed as a Habesha, in sandals instead of the Sudanese jellabiya. I called out in Tigrigna, "Hello, brother," and he answered back. I was relieved. Though we shared little language, he guided me to a woman who sold Habesha food. I paid for both our meals as thanks. Then he pointed me toward Um Gulja, a refugee camp outside Gedarif.

When I arrived, armed soldiers checked IDs at the gate. Those without IDs were beaten with sticks. I had no papers. I stayed at the back of the line, thinking about what awaited me. At last, I was the only one left. I stepped forward and, instead of cowering, began speaking to them in English:

"I need to see your officer. I have just arrived from Ethiopia."

They froze, startled. One soldier saluted me. They led me through rows of soldiers to a raised chair where an officer waited. He questioned me in English, showing off his fluency to his men. "Is your mother here? Your father?" I said no to each question. His soldiers admired him for knowing the words; they admired me for speaking back to him with confidence.

Finally, he asked, "Are you hungry?"

"Yes," I replied. Food was brought, but I asked if it was Muslim food. When they said yes, I refused. "I am Christian," I said. The officer turned to his men and declared that I was a hard-core Ethiopian, educated and unbending. For a moment, I thought I had doomed myself, but instead, they respected me. He ordered that I be taken to men who owned a bakery.

They gave me bread and tea and offered me work selling bread in the camp, just as I had carried water in Hamdayt. I refused, not wanting to be trapped in the same cycle. Instead, I sought other work. Eventually, I registered to pick cotton.

As I stood waiting, I spotted a familiar figure across the street: a bearded man, shirt untucked like the Sudanese. I approached cautiously. "Are you Jefri?"

He looked up. "Are you Zinah?"

It was him Jefri, my Aya Muluken's friend from Debre Markos. Relief washed over me. I shared my story with him, and he responded with kindness. He introduced me to friends, and for the first time in months, I felt safe. I even took my watch from hiding and wore it again.

Jefri once tried to arrange for me to return to Ethiopia and fight. The man we were supposed to meet never arrived, and that gave me time to think. The Derg, the EPRP, the EPLF, the TPLF, and even AESM all claimed to be socialist yet fought each other. If I could not even understand why, how could I claim to liberate Ethiopia?

My father's words returned to me: "Son, be careful. Do not let someone use you to prod another's pain."

I realized then: before I could help liberate my country, I had to liberate myself from ignorance. I had only a high school education. If I wanted to lead or even survive with purpose, I needed more. I needed to go beyond high school.

A Fall at the Cinema

Life in Gedarif was never without its dangers, sometimes in ways I least expected. One evening, I joined the long line outside the cinema, eager to watch a film. To my left was the solid wall of the building, and to my right, an open storm drainage trench lined with stone and concrete. The crowd pressed and swayed, and suddenly a shove from the front sent me stumbling. I tripped, fell backwards, and the edge of the trench struck the back of my head and I fainted.

When I began to regain consciousness, I heard voices around me: three men, debating what to do. Some words were muffled; others clear enough. They wanted to take me to the hospital. As my vision cleared and my strength returned, I shook my head. "No," I said. I got up, brushed myself off, and walked back to the line.

Later that night, my friends noticed blood on my shirt. Alarmed, they asked what had happened. When I told them, they were baffled. "Why go back to the movie instead of home or the hospital?"

I answered simply: "It wouldn't have made a difference. Life has to go on."

At the time, it felt like a small act of stubbornness. Looking back now, I see it as an early lesson: falls happen, sometimes without warning, sometimes leaving scars. But what matters is not fall, it is the getting back up.

That night in Gedarif foreshadowed many chapters of my life, from the day I fell off a pole as a young installer to the moment I lost my job at the height of my career. Each time, I chose the same path: rise, keep going, and never let the setback write the ending.

One day, sitting at a café with other refugees, Sudanese security officers came and forced us into an extended Land Rover and took us to a nearby police detention area. There was no explanation why we were getting rounded up. There were many others in my age group. I asked others if they knew why we were forced and held here. They told me the Sudanese do this often to harass the refugees and extort. They don't even have our names, just our looks and the way we dress. Once they gather as many people as they can, they take us to court, and a judge will fine everyone a large fee. Those who pay are released, and those who cannot pay will be taken to the farm and work for a minimum of one month. Sudan was better because my life was not in danger, nor will I be tortured, but I am not willing to be enslaved. How could I be on the run for the freedom of the oppressed and lose my freedom for myself? This became an additional reason why Sudan is not for me.

More refugees arrived in Gedarif each week. My friend Zena and I ran into each other. I could not believe he was still alive. He was in jail when I left, but somehow, he survived. We first passed each other in the street. I looked back, and he looked back, and I went to him to ask if that was really him. At the same time, I was happy that he was there. It was another confirmation that the resistance had collapsed. Some gave up the struggle and dreamed of Europe or Australia. I had no such path. For me, Africa was the limit. But I had heard of Kenya, a country independent from Britain, where English was spoken, where perhaps I could study again.

Jefri and his girlfriend Fantu shared the same idea. Together, we set our eyes on Nairobi. The Sudan chapter of my life was ending. Ahead lay a new road, one that glimmered faintly with hope.

Reflection

Sudan was both a refuge and a trap. It gave me distance from Ethiopia's terror, but also showed me the dangers of dependency, betrayal, and false hopes. In Hamdayt and Gedarif, I learned that survival was not only about escaping death. It was about reclaiming dignity. Selling water, hiding my true self, outwitting liars and thieves, these became my daily trials. Yet in the midst of it all, I discovered that my struggle was no longer only against the Derg, but against ignorance itself. Liberation, I realized, begins not with a rifle, but with knowledge.

And so, my journey turned toward Kenya not as a soldier, but as a student seeking the light at the end of a long tunnel.

The Long Road to Kenya

Jefri went ahead and secured a place for us in Khartoum. I joined my friends there and stayed for three weeks while we prepared for the next stage of our journey. Eventually, we bought train tickets from Khartoum to Wau.

In Sudan, there were no reserved seats for such trips. Tickets were sold far beyond the number of seats available. Some stood the whole way, others sat on the floor, and still others clung to the back of the train. There were no scheduled stops, no bathrooms, and the trip would take five days and four nights. We disguised Fantu as a local woman to avoid suspicion.

We rationed what little food we carried: bananas first, then oranges, saving the sardines for last. Jefri and Fantu managed to find seats, but I stood for hours. Eventually, I saw people crawling out onto the back of the train, and I followed. It was dangerous that two people fell off during the journey. At one point, a fire broke out, and we had to evacuate until it was put out. The danger of the journey is heightened by the fire and falling passengers, showing the dire conditions.

When we arrived in Wau, a tall Southern Sudanese man who was interested in Fantu during the ride insisted on taking us to his home. His persistence alarmed us. Pretending to agree, we slipped away and searched for transport to Juba. Jefri and I left Fantu at a truck and went to look for food, only to run into the same man. He grabbed Jefri and demanded, "Where is the girl?" Our fears were confirmed. His intentions were sinister. Jefri quickly handed him money, and he let us go.

We boarded a truck for Juba, a three-day journey. The driver, likely intoxicated, sped recklessly down the unpaved road. Branches whipped past us as we ducked for cover. At one point, he hit a deep pothole, and the truck flipped. Jefri was thrown into the grass, but miraculously unharmed. The two Scottish couples traveling with us seemed unfazed. The woman in the cab even remarked, "I hope he has insurance." To me, it was pure madness. We were lucky to survive.

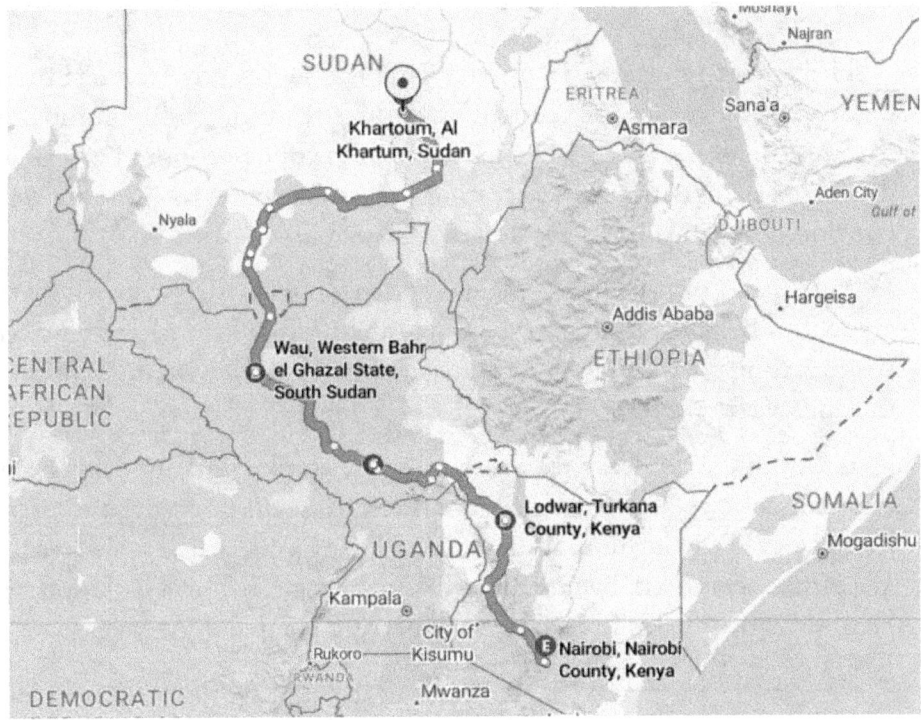

The one-month journey from Khartoum to Nairobi. We stopped in Juba for 10 days, and we were also detained in Nairobi for 3 days, with the rest of the time on the road.

When we finally reached Juba, we rented a small hotel room. To find trustworthy people, we decided to visit the university, reasoning that someone educated would be more reliable. As we wandered, we heard a radio broadcast in Amharic from Deutsche Welle. We followed the sound to a room, where I saw a bearded man in a jellabiya lying on a bed. Startled, he rose. I waved and explained that we were Ethiopians looking for help.

Soon, another man entered. He questioned us closely, probing every detail of our past. When I mentioned Bahrdar in 1966 (Ethiopian calendar), he asked who I knew. I told him about my father, a Woreda administrator, and the student protests where demonstrating students shouted, "Mengesha city dog." To my shock, he said: "I am that, Mengesha."

He had been my father's superior, later the deputy governor of Eritrea, before defecting. Now he lectured on courses at the university in Juba. At first, his friend treated us with suspicion, even condescension. Later on he drove up in a Land Rover, fearing we might be assassins. But once convinced by our story, they allowed us to stay.

Mengesha contacted sympathetic Sudanese military officers who were graduates of Harar Military Academy in Ethiopia, who issued us travel passes stating we were going to Kenya for the 1981 New Year. With these in hand, we found Pakistani truck drivers willing to take us south.

Crossing the border was no easier. At one checkpoint, our papers were rejected, and we were detained for three days. Surprisingly, the police treated us well, giving us food and even allowing me to bathe at a water tap. We earned their trust. Eventually, we were brought before a senior officer. Friendly and kind, he listened to our story and granted us passage.

At last, we crossed into Kenya. It will be my home for the coming months.

Reflection

That journey from Khartoum to Kenya tested every ounce of endurance and vigilance I had left. Five nights on a train, evading predatory men, surviving reckless drivers, and placing my fate in the hands of strangers, all of it underscored the fragility of my existence. Yet with each trial, I learned something crucial: survival was not just about slipping past danger, but

86

about reading people, seizing small opportunities, and trusting my instincts.

Sudan had been a tunnel, dark, narrow, uncertain. Crossing into Kenya felt like stepping toward the light at the end of it. For the first time, I saw the possibility of education, of growth, of rebuilding myself not just as a survivor, but as someone with a future.

Chapter 6 - Nairobi: Holding on to Hope

Once we arrived in Nairobi, we searched for other Ethiopians who could help us understand how to survive there. The city, though a refuge from the terror of Ethiopia, felt like another battle. We went to the UNHCR office and requested asylum. An attorney was assigned to us, and we were given temporary accommodation in a hotel for nine days, along with a small stipend for food. Kenyan immigration authorities issued us a PI notice (prohibited immigrant), which allowed us to stay only 30 days at a time, subject to constant renewal. Every step we took felt like flowing water. Just barely surviving but never truly arriving.

Life was fragile. The UNHCR offered me 150 Kenyan shillings per month (about $15 USD). My friends were treated as a family unit, so they qualified for a larger stipend. We found a place to rent in Kawangware, a crowded suburb of Nairobi. The room we rented was no more than 10 by 10 feet, and it felt as if the walls were closing in on me. We had two beds, some pots, a small gas stove, and a radio to hear the news, including Amharic broadcasts from Ethiopia, a daily reminder of the world we had left behind.

We lived simply, sometimes barely living. Every day we cooked injera from corn flour with lentil stew. Once a week, I bought two eggs, which we shared among the three of us. Once a month, on payday, we bought a kilo of beef from the butcher. Some days, we were lucky to split half a loaf of bread with a bottle of Coke. Hunger was always present, but it wasn't just the physical hunger over me. It was the hunger for a future and for education.

I came to Nairobi with the hope of continuing my education. But I had no clear path, no roadmap. I began writing letters, dozens of them. I wrote to humanitarian organizations, to anyone who might be able to help me. Each letter started with an introduction explaining who I was and that I needed help to continue school. I spent two months wandering through

Nairobi, seeing the faces of the world's lost souls in the crowded office lobbies of Save the Children and World Vision.

One day, when I returned to the office, a man rushed out and waved me over. He had read my letter and wanted to help. His eyes were curious but kind, and something about his manner gave me hope. He asked me to explain my situation. I explained that my education had been disrupted, and that although I had finished high school, I doubted the quality of what I had learned because of the revolution. I proposed starting again in grade 11, giving myself two years to prepare properly for university. He agreed and offered to cover tuition. His words were a light in my darkest hours.

I enrolled at Wakulima Secondary School, a modest institution, but one that gave me the chance to rebuild. I had no textbooks, but I took every course I could, eager to learn.

Later, I took the UNHCR exam to evaluate refugees for scholarships. The exam was intense, but I pushed through with urgency. To my surprise, I scored well and was offered a three-year scholarship to study at the Kenyan Polytechnic in Nairobi, starting in August.

But while I prepared for school, life grew harder. Refugees began leaving for the United States, Europe, or Australia. Jefri and Fantu applied for asylum and left for Dallas, Texas. I was left behind, alone, without the proper support system I had some to rely on. The room we shared was tight for three people. The cramped space in Ngara, a bustling Nairobi neighborhood, was nothing like the days spent with friends. It was walking distance to the city saving me the cost of bus rides. My friends were kind and I did not have to pay rent. The space was so tight but convenient in so many ways

Later, my friends left for North America, and I shared a room with new friends, both kind and supportive. They had stipends. I had little. Still, I endured. Then, my name appeared on a list at the UNHCR office. I was called for interviews at the U.S. Embassy. After three interviews, I was approved for refugee resettlement.

Now I faced a choice: Kenya Polytechnic or America. Polytechnic meant three years of study in a country where I could not legally work. America meant starting over with freedom to work, study, and live. America meant freedom.

I chose America. On July 10, 1982, I boarded Pan Am Airlines bound for the United States.

Reflection

Nairobi was both hardship and hope. I slept beneath a bed, lived on lentils and eggs, and wrote letters to strangers begging for education. Yet, despite all the struggles, I discovered persistence. Even in hunger, I found ways to search for books and knowledge. Even in exile, I dreamed bigger.

The city taught me that when doors close, you must build your own and knock until someone opens. Nairobi was not the end of my journey. It was the waiting room before the next chapter.

Part III: Life in the USA

Chapter 7 – First Steps in America

That journey began on July 10, 1982, when I boarded a Pan Am flight in Nairobi. I was nervous but determined. The next day, I set foot at JFK Airport in New York, a place so vast it made my head spin. Announcements echoed in English, a language I could follow but not yet master. The sound of moving luggage, rolling carts, and hurried voices formed a constant chorus.

A man met me to guide me to my connecting flight to Dallas. He asked about my luggage. "All I have is this bag," I said, holding my small carry-on. He looked surprised. But for me, everything I owned fits inside it. Memories, clothes, and remnants of a life I had fought to survive.

As the plane descended into Dallas, I looked out the window, curious to see Texas. I saw countless blue circles behind houses. Only later did I learn they were swimming pools. It felt surreal, luxury made visible in every backyard.

On July 11, 1982, I landed at Dallas/Fort Worth Airport. Jefri, Fantu, and their roommate were waiting. We embraced. After ten months apart, we were reunited.

The drive from the airport revealed highways wider than anything I had ever imagined, lined with cars of every shape and size. Houses were enormous, spread far apart, with manicured lawns and glowing lights. Nothing like the crowded huts or narrow streets I had known in Ethiopia or Sudan.

When we arrived at their apartment, I was stunned. There was a living room with sofas, a television, a fully equipped kitchen, and two bedrooms with private bathrooms. It was all mine. No pots hidden under beds. No sleeping beneath them either.

Even the air felt different. The Texas summer heat pressed down on me, but the nights were bright with electric lights, streets glowing as if stars had descended to earth. It was strange to see so many cars and almost no one walking. The days stretched long until 9:00 PM. It was still light.

I was awed, but uneasy too. Everything was new: food, culture, even the way strangers smiled politely without knowing me. Beneath the amazement, one question repeated in my mind: How long will it be before I can stand on my own? When can I work? When can I start school?

Reflection

Coming to America was like stepping from the shadows into the sunlight. Only days before, I was sleeping under a bed in Nairobi. Now, I have my own place in Dallas. Yet comfort alone was not enough. Arrival was not the end of my struggle. It was only the beginning. The U.S. offered freedom, but it also demanded responsibility. I knew that to succeed, I had to move quickly from survival to self-sufficiency. The boy who once disguised himself as a farmer to escape the Derg was now a man who needed to prove, with effort and learning, that he belonged.

Settling In the USA

I shared a small bedroom with Jefri and Fantu, grateful to have family nearby. Many others from Kenya and Sudan were also beginning to settle in Dallas. Some called to welcome me, and others came to visit, creating a small but steady circle of support in this new land.

Even simple things felt unfamiliar. In Ethiopia, time was measured by the sun, sunrise to sunset. In America, days ran midnight to midnight. At first, I struggled to understand how 1:00 AM still in the middle of the night could be considered "the next day." Summer days stretched to fourteen hours while nights lasted only ten. Coming from the equator, where daylight and darkness were almost equal year-round, I found myself constantly disoriented.

Language added another challenge. Americans spoke with accents I had never heard before, mixing slang that textbooks had not prepared me for. When someone said, "I'm gonna go," I puzzled over it until I could ask someone later what it meant. Once, in an elevator, a man greeted me casually with "What's up!" I pretended not to hear until I could inquire. Even small greetings carried hidden codes. Currency was just as confusing. Nickels, dimes, quarters, and "bucks" all seemed designed to trip me up.

Catholic Charities was a lifeline for refugees. Jefri took me there to register, guiding me through every step as he once did in Gedarif. They gave me $150 to help with first expenses. Jefri, who was already working at the Dallas Times Herald, introduced me to his supervisor. On July 26, I was hired.

In the first week of my arrival in Dallas at the Trinity River bridge.

I went to the interview in the only clothes I owned, jeans and a short-sleeved shirt. I did not yet realize that the casual questions they asked were part of the assessment itself. Soon, I was working alongside Jefri, riding the bus with him to and from work every day. Two weeks later, I received my first paycheck: $326. I skipped to the bank with joy, proud to deposit my first earnings in America.

I contributed to the rent and groceries, but I also saved aggressively. My lunch was the same every day: two slices of bread with scrambled eggs in between. After a while, it reminded me of the endless lentil stew in Nairobi. Yet I endured it in the name of saving, discipline shaping my days as much as survival had in Africa.

At the Times Herald, each employee received a daily copy of the newspaper. I studied the classified ads, especially the used car section. Within three months, I had saved enough to buy a small stick-shift car in downtown. The fuel gauge didn't work, but I relied on the trip meter. Owning a manual car felt like a skill I could someday carry back to Ethiopia.

Cultural customs often caught me off guard. A young woman smiled at me, and I assumed it was an invitation to visit. When I almost walked towards her door, she went inside and closed the door. At McDonald's, I invited another girl for a drink. She asked for root beer. Certain it contained alcohol, I insisted she was mistaken only to later realize root beer had no alcohol. Worst of all was the time I tried to take food from a woman's plate, telling her she didn't need it because she was "already fat." I had no idea how cutting that word was in American culture. After these missteps, I bought a book called Talking American to keep myself out of further trouble.

Stopped in the Dark

Once I had my driver's license, I felt free to go anywhere. One evening I visited my friend Birhane at the store where he worked. On my way back, I noticed a car flashing red and blue lights behind me. I thought he wanted to pass, so I changed lanes. But he changed lanes too, staying right behind me.

Another driver shouted, "He wants you to pull over!" I froze. "Pull over?" To me, a pullover was a sweater. I assumed the car wanted to talk, so I stopped on the shoulder and got out.

Suddenly, the man screamed: "Get back in the car!" His flashlight blinded me. That was when I realized: he was a police officer.

"Put your hands on the steering wheel!" he barked.

I complied immediately. Coming from a country where soldiers could shoot without warning, I dared not move.

"License and registration!" he demanded next.

I froze. "Your directions are conflicting," I said carefully. "You told me to put my hands on the wheel, but now you want me to reach into my pocket."

He kept yelling, so I slowly retrieved my license. After a tense few minutes, he berated me for a broken brake light: "I almost hit you!"

I knew he was exaggerating because why would he follow up too close and yet, one of the brake lights still work. He was just looking to catch someone doing something wrong. But I dared not argue. His hand rested on his gun the whole time.

He issued a ticket. That word confused me, too. A "ticket" was something you bought for the movies, the bus, or a flight but not something that fined you for breaking a law. The driver's manual had not explained what flashing lights behind your car meant, nor what to do when a police officer stopped you.

That night, I mailed the $26 fine, checking the "not guilty" option with a money order. I had learned my first lesson in American authority the hard way: flashing red and blue lights meant stop immediately. Since then, I checked my brake lights before every drive.

Reflection:

This moment taught me two things at once: the cultural gap, and the power imbalance when authority wields anger instead of guidance. To the officer, I was just another careless driver. To me, I was still learning a new country's rules. Survival meant adapting quickly, even when the rules weren't in the manual.

Facing Hatred on Gaston Avenue

I was still new to America, learning streets and social cues, when my friends Addisu, Hailu, Birhane, and I decided to go to a bar on Gaston Avenue. We took a seat, waited, but no one came to serve us. Eventually, we had to go up to the bartender ourselves, only to be met with cold stares and a server who handed us drinks with contempt written on his face.

A man came over and dangled a keychain in front of my face, the letters KKK gleaming under the dim lights. I tried to ignore him, sensing that he wanted to provoke a fight.

"Do you know what this means?" he sneered.

"No," I said calmly.

"It means, n***** go to hell."

In that moment I understood exactly where we were and how much danger we were in. Other patrons were watching us closely, some with silent approval of his actions. One wrong word could have turned the room against us. So instead of feeding his fire, I defused it. I said, "We are students from Africa, just here temporarily. My name is Mike."

He turned, raised his voice, and announced to the whole room, "They're okay. They're students from Africa." The tension broke. We left quietly, unharmed but sobered.

A few days later, I confronted him on a city bus. "You were a racist that day in the bar. I played dumb and pretended I didn't know what you meant, but I did. I wasn't going to fall into your trap. You need to know I am not going anywhere. I am here to stay. If you have a problem, now you face me man to man."

His bravado melted. He apologized, and admitted, "I was being stupid."

I told him, "Yes, you were. And I was smarter than you."

That day I reminded him and myself that dignity, patience, and timing can be stronger than hate. There are moments when it is right to confront prejudice directly. Moments when it is wiser to study it from a distance. Moments when the best choice is to keep it at bay. Knowing the difference has been a lesson I have carried through my life.

The Words I Carried

My first job was as a janitor. If my friends did the work, who was I to feel it beneath me? I knew it was temporary. It is not where I started that mattered, it is where I was aiming to be. Since I was seventeen, I had carried Desiderata like a compass in my pocket. Its lines became my guide through foreign lands, uncertain jobs, and the shifting fortunes of time.

When I felt like a stranger in America, a fish out of water, I held on to the words:

"Beyond a wholesome discipline, be gentle with yourself. You are a child of the universe no less than the trees and the stars; you have a right to be here."

Those words reminded me that I belonged, even when my accent, my skin, or my unfamiliar ways marked me as an outsider.

Later, when I worked jobs that felt beneath my ambition, or when I doubted the path I was on, I remembered:

"Enjoy your achievements as well as your plans. Keep interested in your own career, however humble; it is a real possession in the changing fortunes of time."

I took pride not just in where I was going, but in the step I was standing on.

Over the years, the poem became a mentor, a prayer, and a reminder that my dignity was never conditional. It told me I had a right to be here, to strive, to dream, and to grow. My best days were just ahead of me over the next horizon.

Six months later, I was promoted from janitorial work to operating the shredding machine, compacting wastepaper into bales, and even learned to use the forklift. The night shift, 10:00 PM to 6:00 AM, allowed me to attend Richland Community College in the afternoons.

One day, while driving to class, my car broke down in the middle of rush hour. I pushed it off the road and continued walking to class, determined not to be late. By the time I returned, the car was gone. Assuming it was stolen, I called the police. They explained it had been towed for blocking the street and was sitting in the impound lot. My friend next door, Demelash, came to the rescue and helped me push it out after I paid the fee. I was learning, sometimes the hard way, what it meant to be a car owner in America.

At the Times Herald, I impressed my supervisors immediately. On my first day, my production was double that of a man who had been doing the work for four years. Yet, when a better-paying position opened, I was told I lacked "experience." I felt insulted. Was it because I was Black? An immigrant with an accent? America's history of slavery came to mind. I wondered if bias played a role.

It echoed my past. In Humera, Ate Beyene had tried to keep me working by withholding my pay. Woldie had wanted to keep me selling water for him instead of letting me move on. Now, here in America, I want freedom to grow and not to be trapped again. My frustration grew when they overlooked my annual merit increase.

And when I requested a vacation, our manager, Ken, replied, "You can request a vacation, not demand it." I insisted and took my vacation. After returning from a week off, I gave my two-week notice.

I searched in the classified pages of The Dallas Morning News and found a job at El Centro College's Job Training Center. It felt like a step closer to something new, away from laboring jobs. There, I worked as a Building Crafts Helper cleaning classrooms, preparing the building for the day, and assisting with repairs under my supervisor, Julius, and my coworker, Oscar.

But after my car troubles and missing classes, I realized I needed another vehicle. The pace was brutal. I dropped out of school temporarily and picked up a second job to save faster. My schedule became brutal. I worked at El Centro from 5:00 AM to 1:00 PM, then drove to my second job at a gas station from 2:00 PM to 10:00 PM. By the time I got home and fell asleep, it was nearly 11:00 PM. At 4:00 AM, the alarm rang again. Five hours of sleep became normal. After three months, I was completely exhausted, sometimes dozing at stoplights until honking cars woke me. One morning, I didn't hear the alarm at all, and the school doors were late to open.

The gas station job paid the minimum wage of $3.65 an hour, but it nearly cost me more than it gave. One Tuesday night, a man asked for a pack of Pall Mall Gold cigarettes. As I turned to hand it over, I found myself staring down the barrel of a gun. He screamed at me to open the cash register, grabbed the $84 inside, and ran. My boss was almost cheerful, saying he was "happy" it was less than $100. The next day, he took me to a bar to celebrate. At the door, a woman asked who I was, and he told her, "He's my employee. He got robbed yesterday." She asked who did it, and he sneered: "Who else? Nigg**s."

I was stunned. After that, I resigned without notice.

I was working 56 hours a week at minimum wage, standing the whole time, robbed at gunpoint, and employed by a racist boss. I had dropped out of Richland, lost my second job, and knew I had to find a new path.

One afternoon at El Centro, I noticed people climbing poles. Curious, I asked what they were doing. "Cable TV training," someone explained. I went straight to investigate. That single moment opened the door to the future. Standing there, watching them scale those poles, I realized this was the road to a new life.

Reflection

Looking back, those first years in Dallas tested me in every possible way. I learned what it meant to adapt to a new culture, to push through exhaustion, and to face danger and prejudice without breaking. Each setback hardened my resolve. Every insult, every missed opportunity, every long shift became the reason for the fire that drove me forward.

At the time, I could not have imagined where the path would lead. But one thing was clear: I wanted more, more than minimum wage, more than survival. Seeing students climb poles revealed a path, a door to opportunity. I was all ready to walk through it.

Transition

Leaving behind the hardships of survival jobs, I turned toward something I barely understood but felt drawn to immediately: cable television. It was more than training for a new skill. It was a chance to build a future. With nothing to lose and everything to gain, I decided to take the risk.

Opening a New Door

Leaving the Dallas Times Herald was a leap into the unknown. Walking away from a steady paycheck was difficult, but I could not stay where I was undervalued. At El Centro College's Job Training Center, I found both stability and opportunity. By day, I worked as a Building Crafts Helper, by afternoon, I trained for something entirely new.

Since my shift ended at 1:00 PM, I enrolled in the Cable TV Installer program that ran from 3:00 to 6:00 in the afternoons. On the first day, I asked my instructor, John, a simple question:

"What is cable TV?"

He smiled and said, "It is a shielded wire that transmits about fifty channels with full motion, color, and sound. The signal is received on a parabolic dish from satellites in space, in geosynchronous orbit. The field is new. Demand is huge, and the growth potential is untapped. Technicians are needed everywhere.

His words struck me immediately. Driving around town with only a map reminded me of being lost in the Ethiopian countryside with no written directions. Then I read a line in the job description:

"Installer works alone and sometimes with others, under his own self-initiative."

That phrase, "self-initiative," stayed with me and still does to this day.

In this picture, I was on the pole completing a service call.

I came from a country where television belonged to the wealthy. In Ethiopia, TV sets were rare, and those who had them saw only black-and-white images. Programming was limited to a few hours in the morning and evening, mostly government propaganda with a little entertainment sprinkled in. The idea of television being available all day, with fifty different channels, sounded almost unbelievable. Why would anyone even want TV all day long?

What I didn't understand yet was that MTV was all music videos, CNN was all news, and HBO was all movies channels built to satisfy every possible interest. Suddenly, I began to see that cable line was not just wires and boxes, but a revolution in how people lived and connected.

That realization filled me with joy that went far beyond the technical work. I wasn't just running cable lines into homes. I was introducing families to a whole new world of choice and connection. My enthusiasm became part of the installation itself, as much as the wires and fittings I carried.

The training was hands-on. I learned to climb poles, connect lines, and install cable inside homes. John doubted me at first, even mocking me:

"Are you sure you can afford it? It's $360."

He didn't know that my employer had agreed to cover it. I had no excuse to fail, only the choice to succeed.

When the course ended, I faced my first major setback. I was advised to start as a contractor, using my savings to buy tools and a step ladder. But I didn't even own a truck.

When I applied at a contracting company, the hiring manager interviewed me on the spot and then said, "We need to inspect your truck."

My heart sank. I had no truck. But I couldn't say no. We walked out into the parking lot, and he asked, "Which one is your truck?"

I pointed to a blue 1979 Chevette.

He squinted. "I don't see a truck."

"The blue one," I said.

He laughed. "That's a car."

"It does the job of a truck," I replied.

Curious, he followed me to the car. I opened the trunk, showing climbing gear, a toolbox, a power drill, and a six-foot ladder. I even removed the passenger seat to fit the ladder securely inside. He shook his head in disbelief. "How did you get this in here?"

"Carefully," I said. "And I don't need a 28-foot extension ladder. There isn't a pole in Dallas. I can't climb. The day you find one, you can fire me."

He laughed. "You're hired."

On my first jobs, I quickly discovered how skeptical people were. A woman glanced past me toward the street and asked, "Where's your truck?"

I told her, "There is no need for a truck. This little blue car is all I need."

But the work was scarce. Small jobs brought only twelve dollars. Worse, I had already spent $1,500 on tools, and rent was due. My savings were gone. With only $136 in the bank and $210 rent due, I needed income fast.

So, one Friday morning, I decided to try taxi driving. I upgraded my license, went to City Hall for a permit, and completed a three-hour exam. Passing surprised the clerks.

Next, I went to the Yellow Cab office with my paperwork. The owner asked for a $250 security deposit. I wrote him a check I knew wouldn't clear before Monday, then rented a cab and drove straight to Love Field Airport. By Monday morning, before the bank opened, I was waiting at the door with $400 cash to deposit.

In less than three days, I earned more than I ever had in America. Driving a taxi was good money and easy work. At night, I joined other Ethiopians at the taxi stand, chatting while we waited for fares. But even as I enjoyed the income, I refused to let go of my dream. I drove a taxi late in the afternoons and evenings, but during the day I slept beside the phone, afraid to miss a call from the cable company. Back in those days, there were no answering machines, no voicemail, no text messages, and no one home to take the call for me. If I miss the call, I may not get another chance.

One day, the call came around 11:00 AM. I had my interview and was hired at Warner Amex for $6.00 an hour. When I shared the news with my fellow cab drivers, they laughed. "You gave up taxi money for that?" they asked. "You'll make less than half of what you earn now and do all that hard work."

I told them, "Taxi is good cash, and less physical demand, but it has no future. Cable has growth and I love the work. Let's compare notes in five years."

Years later, I became Vice President of Technical Operations at one of the largest Fortune 500 telecommunications companies, responsible for four departments, more than 1,060 employees, and a $60 million annual budget. Many of those men were still driving taxis.

When I was a field technician, I loved the freedom of working outdoors. The Texas heat, the splinters from climbing poles, and the suffocating attics that sometimes reached 150 degrees didn't deter me. The insulation made my skin itch and my throat cough, but I still approached each assignment with a sense of adventure.

One afternoon, I was returning to the office early to drop off paperwork and park the truck. My supervisor, Ron Monroe, happened to be leaving. Usually, he didn't see me at the end of the day, but this time he stopped and asked, "Did you finish your route?"

Surprised, I answered, "Is that an option?"

Later, I learned that some technicians left early, passing unfinished jobs back to dispatch for others to pick up. But I never expected anyone else to do my work. I did every assignment I was given, and sometimes I helped others who could not finish their work.

This marked the true beginning of my career. From 1984 onward, I poured myself into learning the business. Every wire, every pole, every installation detail. Step by step, I rose from installer to supervisor, manager, and eventually Division Vice President. What had started with a leap of faith and a small step ladder shoved into a little blue car became a lifelong career of nearly forty years.

Chapter 8 – Building a Career, Building a Life

The years of struggle in Dallas, the exhaustion, the culture shock, grueling jobs, sleepless nights, and even danger had forged in me a resilience that no setback could break. Finding cable TV was not just a job. It was a turning point where survival gave way to purpose. With my small ladder shoved into a blue Chevette, I stepped into an industry that was itself just beginning to grow.

The last company I worked for had $120 billion in annual revenue, serving over 50 million internet customers and more than 12 million video customers. Compare that to the modest beginning of my installer days: $30 million in revenue, 3 million video subscribers, and 64,000 cable connections in Dallas. Today, broadband, including fiber optics, reaches over 1.2 million homes. I had been in the right place at the right time, faithful to a vision that would define my career.

Building Skills Beyond Tools

Even while working full-time, I enrolled in classes. The first focus was English. I knew that I was still alone and could never determine whether my hands could lead to advancement.

Languages had always come naturally. In ninth grade in Ethiopia, I studied French and earned high marks with little effort. In Sudan, I picked up Arabic, pronouncing words so accurately that when I wore a jellabiya, I could blend in with locals. In Kenya, I worked on English, and in America, I sharpened it further. I listened to talk shows in the car, repeated phrases from TV comedies, and practiced the rhythm behind the words.

I even bought tapes and CDs, inspired by Arnold Schwarzenegger, to soften my accent. At work, every conversation, face-to-face with customers or over the radio with dispatchers, became practice. Slowly, my fluency earned me respect.

In those early years, I often turned to self-help books and cassette tapes for guidance. Brian Tracy provided tools for discipline and goal-setting. Les Brown inspired hunger for success. I did not always have mentors at my side, but these voices became my invisible teachers. They taught me that success begins in the mind long before it shows up in a career. I carried those lessons into every promotion and later passed them on to those I mentored.

The next set of promotions I got was inspired by stories I heard from Les Brown. He told a story about how he wanted to be a DJ at a radio station, but they told him there were no job openings. They even told him not to come to that radio station ever again. One day, the real DJ missed work because he was drunk the night before. They looked for Les Brown, and he was there. They asked him to fill in for the DJ. He did such a great job, they called the DJ and told him he was fired. In the jobs I wanted, I looked for gaps I could fill so that I could grow. I was inspired by Les Brown, and the stories he told about himself resonated with me.

Breaking Into Service Work

My first role as an installer gave me stability, but I was restless. The next step was a service technician, but it required "experience." How could I gain experience without first having the job? I came up with an idea.

I noticed that weekend absenteeism was high. Supervisors had two bad choices: overloading the remaining service techs or reschedule calls, leaving customers angry. I offered a third option: "I'll take the routes on my days off, unpaid, just for the experience."

At first, he hesitated. "You don't have service experience," I answered, "I install the service and know when things aren't working. I've even earned a plaque for quality installations. What do you lose by giving me a route? Worst-case, I'll call for help. But refusing me still leaves angry customers."

He gave me a route for fourteen jobs. I completed them all including one where the TV picture kept rolling until I discovered the horizontal adjustment knob on the back of the set. From then on, I no longer had to ask. On my off days, supervisors came looking for me.

Within weeks, without applying, I was offered the service technician position with a raise. I joined the Society of Cable Telecommunications Engineers (SCTE), enrolled in electronics classes, and studied training tapes. Every job became a step forward.

The Trailer Park Years

After about three years in the United States, my ambition grew restless. I had little money and had not finished college, but I decided I would own my own home, no matter how humble. I didn't want to remain a tenant. Even if it was only an RV, I would make it mine.

An opportunity came through the Ethiopian community. A trailer had been offered for donation, and when most of the others dismissed it as beneath them, and they did not know, I saw it as my starting point. I drove sixty miles to Whitewright, Texas, to see it, a 68-foot by 14-foot mobile home with two bedrooms, two bathrooms, a kitchen, and a living room. It was exactly what I needed. For $625, I had it towed to Mesquite, paying $125/month for the land, water included.

People warned me: "It's dangerous," they said. "Motorcycle gangs like the Hell's Angels live in those parks. A Black man like you could be lynched."

But I told myself: "I had crossed rivers infested with crocodiles, lived in refugee camps, and survived war. I had not come to America to cower. I had come to the land of the free and the home of the brave."

To make my point, I went to an Army surplus store, bought fatigues, dummy grenades, and a shooting-range poster. On the poster, in bold letters above a bullet-pocked target, I wrote: Go ahead, make my day.

I practiced with my brand-new Smith & Wesson .357, and when my friend Teshome moved in, he bought the same model. We practiced together at the range and made sure people saw us coming and going, pistols and ammo in hand. We lived there for four years in peace, saved $17,000, and purchased a proper home in Dallas, debt-free.

Those years were not just about survival. They were about proving myself in a world wary of my presence.

One Saturday, my supervisor, Stan, invited us to his ranch. "Bring your gun," he said. "We'll do some target shooting."

A coworker whispered a warning: "Don't go. It's a Ku Klux Klan rally."

I laughed. "A rally? Then I want to see how they rally. I thought they were secretive."

So, I went fully prepared. Demelash came with me. At the ranch, I wore my revolver in its holster, ammunition ready. Ronny, our lead technician, was already there drinking Budweiser when he saw me. He looked me up and down, laughed, and said, "A small guy like you, with a big gun like that? What are you doing with that?"

He threw his beer can as far as he could and said, "Let's see if you can shoot that."

I have practiced for this moment thousands of times. I pulled the revolver with my left hand, Western style, and in one smooth motion shot the can. It leapt into the air, spinning. His jaw dropped. "Do it again, do it again," he said, stunned.

I smiled. "No. I don't waste bullets."

It was the perfect ending. If I missed, I would lose the respect I had just earned. By walking away, I left the moment unforgettable and mine.

Those years in the trailer park taught me how to carve respect out of unlikely places. To some, it was a risky choice. To me, it was the foundation of a life. That trailer, that revolver, that patch of rented land were not symbols of poverty. They were proof that even with little, I could build a life of my own choosing.

This picture was taken when I lived at the trailer park. I dressed in military clothes from an Army surplus store. This helped me ward off potential problems.

Becoming a Line Technician

After a year and a half as a service technician, I was ready for the next challenge: line technician. This role was different from service work. I no longer raced across town to appease frustrated customers, nor hauled ladders through alleys and fences. Line technicians maintained the trunk and distribution lines, amplifiers, power supplies, and the backbone of the network. We drove boom trucks and kept entire neighborhoods connected.

Once again, I created my own path. Two generous mentors agreed to train me. On my days off, I rode with them, followed every instruction, and did the work. I asked for one favor: to be the one who called dispatch with updates. Each radio broadcast went to supervisors, managers, and the chief technician. My accent made me stand out, and soon everyone recognized my voice. By the time a posting opened, my interview was little more than a formality. I got the job.

The work came with challenges. Outages didn't wait for daylight. One night at 2:00 AM, I was restoring service at an apartment complex when a woman spotted a Black man climbing a ladder outside her window. She called the police. They arrived quickly, but when they saw my uniform, badge, and truck, they left without incident. It was a reminder that my presence sometimes carried risks my coworkers never faced.

Not everyone welcomed me into the role. Once I was assigned as a Line Technician, I was paired with a veteran employee who was asked to train me. From the start, his tone was clipped, his instructions impatient.

One morning, as I waited in his truck for us to leave, I picked up a thick binder lying on the seat. I thought it was a technical manual, something I could study while I had a quiet moment. Instead, it was full of racist jokes with pages and pages targeting every ethnicity that wasn't white, but especially Iranians. My stomach turned. In that instant, his attitude toward me became clear.

I could have reported him to HR. It would have cost him his job or at least a formal reprimand. But I chose not to. For me, it wasn't about punishing him. It was about understanding him. I watched how he moved through the day, who he sat with in meetings, and who he laughed with in the break room. His prejudice was always there, but I refused to let it poison my own path.

Fourteen years later, I crossed paths with him again, but this time as a Director of Broadband Services, three levels above his position. It was Halloween, and I had dressed proudly in traditional Ethiopian clothes. He looked me up and down and said, "Look who we have, a terrorist in our own backyard."

I smiled and continued with my business. What he never understood was that I loved America perhaps more deeply than he ever could. I was not born into it. I chose it. And with that choice came a commitment to its ideals, even when some of its people failed to live up to them.

Becoming American (1991)

By 1991, I had built stability through hard work and perseverance. But until then, I was still officially a refugee, tied to papers that reminded me of my displacement. That year, I raised my right hand and became a U.S. citizen.

For me, it was more than a ceremony. It was the moment I felt I had a true home again, a country that recognized me not as an outsider but as one of its own. The passport I received later that year was not just a travel document. It was a symbol of belonging, of freedom, of a future finally secured.

Returning Home (1992)

At the end of 1992, I returned to Ethiopia for the first time since leaving. The Derg regime had fallen. The country was in the process of rebuilding.

I had left Ethiopia as a teenage fugitive, scared for my life and unsure if I would live another day. Now, I returned with a child in my arms, a wife at my side, and a mustache on my face. I survived, withstanding every storm across multiple countries. I came back not as the frightened boy who once fled, but as a man who had built a new life against all odds.

The night before my departure, I could not sleep. After I arrived, I could not sleep for several days, overwhelmed with emotion. We talked day and night, my family and I, as they asked about the obstacles I had faced and the dangers I had endured, the very challenges they had long wondered about but never fully known.

But my return was shadowed by tragedy. I had come home after hearing the devastating news that my two youngest brothers, Gebeyaw and Solomon, had been gunned down. Gebeyaw had been away, caught in fighting in the area, and was on his way back. Solomon was sitting quietly inside the house when his life was taken. Their deaths left a wound in me that has never fully healed.

My younger sister, Yewul, and I were on one of my trips back to Ethiopia and on the left when I was four and she was two years old.

When I returned to the U.S., I carried both grief and resolve. I printed photos from my visit and showed them to coworkers who had assumed I came from some "uncivilized" African country. Now they saw asphalt roads, modern cars, high-rise buildings, and my family dressed in dignity and pride. Some stared at the photos, then looked at me again as if I were no longer the same Zinah they had known. Those pictures became a reset button, breaking stereotypes and giving them a glimpse of the Ethiopia I knew.

From then on, I promised myself that I would not wait for tragedy to take me back to Ethiopia. Every trip I made afterward was proactive, a choice to stay connected to my family, my roots, and my homeland. And I carried with me a conviction: some of us die at home, and some of us survive no matter where we go. But as long as we live, we must do what has to be done, no matter what the risk.

Mastering the Demands of On-Call

Being a line tech came with grueling on-call rotations: from 3:00 PM to 11:00 PM, and then standing by through the night. Most of my coworkers hated it. For me, it was an opportunity. The mornings were free, giving me time to take classes and complete homework.

So, I made a proposal to my supervisor: let me handle the on-call shift permanently. Instead of paying me extra only when I was on rotation, roll the premium into my base wage. He agreed. What others saw as a burden, I turned into a stable schedule and another chance to prove I was dependable.

Opening the Door Through Master Control

Next to the Headend, a small team called Master Control Operators managed commercial insertions, cued tapes, and monitored public access channels.

The least desired shift was 3:00 PM to 11:00 PM, and it became open. Few applied, but I saw an opening. I was already a network maintenance tech, SCTE member, and electronics student. I applied and got the job.

Most operators simply called Headend techs after hours, but I asked them to guide me over the phone so I could fix issues myself. Before long, it became routine. They stopped coming back at night, and I handled the problems.

Then I made a proposal to the three Headend techs, Chip, Brad, and Dave. "Talk to your boss, Bennie. Let me be your on-call tech. I don't need a new title or a raise, just the experience." They agreed. Soon, I was issued a pager and a company truck. I had become the unofficial Headend technician.

From Bench Technician to Chief Engineer

From there, my responsibilities expanded. I became a Bench Technician, repairing and maintaining more than thirty Sony ¾-inch professional video cassette players that aired commercials and public access programming. Each unit demanded precision, and mistakes were not tolerated.

Recognizing my positive attitude, my supervisor sent me to New Jersey for specialized training. Soon after, I trained in Florida to train on Rolm office phone systems, learning to install and move phone lines and data terminals for the billing system at the Chenault office.

Soon, I was promoted to Chief Engineer, responsible for maintaining production studio equipment where a single camera cost $70,000. I also drove the $2 million production truck to live events, including the Mesquite Rodeo.

The workload was heavy. One day, I worked twenty hours straight without meals. Coming home, my family was already asleep. I looked at the staircase, and it felt like a mountain. Too tired to climb, I collapsed on the sofa.

This Picture was taken when I was recognized as Employee of the Month

In Master Control, I was working the second shift so that I could go to school by day and learn the headend job.

No matter the exhaustion, I stayed committed. I wasn't just earning a living. I was building a life: step-by-step, wire-by-wire, decision-by-decision.

Chapter 9 - Crossing Into Leadership

Four months into my role as an installer, I was still absorbing every detail, every wire, every connection. One of the supervisors had taken to calling me "Z, macho man." One afternoon, he surprised me by saying he was ready to promote me to a lead technician.

It was a flattering offer, a quick rise, a chance to stand above my peers. But I paused, thought carefully, and told him no.

"I'm not ready," I said. "I don't know enough yet to lead others. I need to learn first."

The memory of Gedarif came rushing back. I remembered my youthful conviction that I had to free myself from ignorance before I could dream of liberating my country. Leadership without understanding was dangerous. It was, as I told myself, the blind leading the blind. And I refused to take on that kind of responsibility before I was prepared.

So, I declined the promotion and went back to work, dedicating myself to mastery first.

A decade later, the wisdom of that choice revealed itself. By then, I had reached the highest technical rank, strengthened by classroom education and years of hard-earned experience in the field. When I finally became a supervisor, one of my employees muttered under his breath, "He thinks he knows it all."

I only smiled. I sure know enough to be your boss, I thought.

That was the lesson: true leadership is not seized in haste. It is built patiently, with humility and with substance.

After a decade as a frontline employee, I was approached about supervision. I had climbed every technical rank available. Now I stand at a fork in the road: stay at the top of the technical track or enter the unknown world of leadership.

Years of frontline experience had prepared me for the moment when Tony B. and Dave approached me about leading a new Converter Control department. Their confidence in my skills and problem-solving gave me courage. The role came with a pay increase and the opportunity to build my own team. I was excited.

Building My First Team

The first order of business was hiring. Veterans like Patricia and Susan transferred from the warehouse, while Mary continued auditing. I also recommended a candidate I knew personally: Mulugeta.

Tony raised concerns. "He's a job hopper. He won't last."

"I can relate to him," I replied. "He just hasn't found the right job yet. Give him the chance, and he'll stay."

Tony smiled and said, "It's your team. Right or wrong, you'll be held responsible."

Mulugeta was hired. He proved himself to be a dedicated worker and remained with the company for 17 years. That moment taught me an early lesson in leadership: trust your instincts but own the responsibility for your choices.

With guidance from my supervisor, Dave, and input from my team, I transformed a single-page process note into a 37-page procedure manual, streamlining converter handling, reducing service calls, and improving operational efficiency. Customers were happier, technicians were more efficient, and the company was stronger for it.

Reaching for More

After two years, I was promoted to Asset Manager, overseeing all Dallas-area warehouses. But three years into leadership, I began to feel restless again. The work was important, but cable television with its one-way signal was starting to bore me.

The PC and IT industries were booming, and I could sense a change coming. On September 5, 1996, TCI launched high-speed internet in Fremont, California. When I read the news, I ran upstairs to the Plant Manager's office to share it. He dismissed it as irrelevant. But I knew better. Dallas would need to adapt, or risk falling behind.

That dismissal lit a fire in me. At the time, I was studying Radio and TV at East Texas State University, with only 17 hours left to complete my degree. I abandoned it and enrolled instead in the Digital (Computer) Electronics associate program at Eastfield College. Education alone wasn't enough. I needed hands-on experience.

Preparing for the Future

I launched a side business building and repairing personal computers. I advertised in the classifieds: "Technician for hire, $50/hour, or free if I don't fix it." I carried a briefcase filled with diagnostic tools, software, and spare parts, driving the family van from house to house. I built PCs for friends and families, gave them orientations on how to use their new machines, and repaired systems that others thought were beyond saving.

When the phone was quiet, I ran another ad: "Cash for Broken PCs." I bought them cheaply, repaired them, and sold them for a small profit. Money wasn't the goal. I wanted experience. I wanted both the classroom education and the hands-on knowledge to be ready for the moment I knew would come: the launch of high-speed internet in Dallas.

As I predicted, two years later, in July 1998, the position of Technical Operations Manager was posted to lead the rollout of the new internet product. I applied, and there was no contest. I was the only candidate with a combined background of cable television, computer electronics, and proven leadership.

The offer came with a significant increase, but even more importantly, it was the opportunity I had been preparing for. And once again, it was Tony B., the same leader who had first believed in me enough to push me into supervision, who hired me. He told me later he was surprised at how, in just three years, I had not only exceeded expectations in leadership but also mastered a whole new skillset after hours and on weekends.

For me, it was no surprise. It was the payoff of faith and persistence.

Launching High-Speed Internet in Dallas

When I became Technical Operations Manager in 1998, the product was so new that few believed in its promise. Cable television was familiar, but the idea of the internet through a cable line seemed uncertain to many. My job was to make it real.

I recruited and hired technicians, worked with marketing, engineering, and the warehouse. But the resources I received were the ones no one else wanted: old trucks missing spares, expired inspection stickers, and no warehouse staff to handle equipment shipments. I hauled the boxes myself.

Someone once asked, "Where are you going to store all those modems?"

"I'm not storing them," I said. "I'm going to have them installed in customers' homes."

From 6:00 to 8:00 AM, I worked as a warehouse operator. From 8:00 to 10:00, I served as dispatcher. For the rest of the day, I was in my normal duty as the manager: tracking and analyzing productivity, attending meetings, writing reports, coaching employees, and riding with my techs in the field to stay grounded. I refused to fall behind the technology I was helping launch.

Proving Myself the Hard Way

In Arlington, I once encountered a new hire, an IT-savvy office worker, frozen at the bottom of a training pole. To show him, I strapped climbing gear to my office clothes and scaled it. My crew cheered, urging me to touch the top.

I climbed too far this time, losing balance with no wires to guide me, and fell from the very top. Bones shattered, chest ruptured, spine compressed. Dizzy and swollen, I could barely walk. In the hospital, when asked if I wanted painkillers, I said, "I need to feel where it hurts. When the pain is gone, I'll know I'm healed."

I refused Workers' Comp writing across the check, "This body is not for sale." Ten days later, I returned with my arm in a cast and a limp.

At the warehouse, Chuck asked me for "a hand." Furious, I kicked the box across the floor. "I can't give you a hand," I told him, "But I can give you a foot." He finally understood.

That stubborn resilience didn't go unnoticed. My boss, Wayne, soon promoted me to Advanced Services Manager, preparing me for the next wave: Voice over IP.

EWOC: Holding Contractors Accountable

As the customer base grew past 20,000, contractors became necessary. Some billed for work not done. I devised EWOC (Email Work Order Confirmation): a technician could only close a job by sending an email confirming the modem was provisioned and the account created.

The system became company parlance: "Did you EWOC your job?" Fraud decreased, accountability increased, and soon I trained other managers on the process. Over time, my role shifted toward advisor as teams were reorganized.

Meeting Anthony Hayes

Then came the turning point. TCI was sold to AT&T Broadband, and with it came new leadership. One day, my boss, Dollie, introduced me to a young man in a polo shirt.

"Hi Zinah," she said, "this is Anthony. He's interviewing for a job."

I shook his hand, wishing him luck. Later, I learned he was Anthony Hayes, Vice President of Technical Operations, and I would soon report directly to him.

Anthony Hayes had a rare gift. He saw through people like an X-ray. In me, he saw ambition and energy not yet spent. He designed a bold plan: consolidate the 19 dispatch groups across video, internet, and voice into one operation.

Director of Broadband Services

Anthony Hayes promoted me to Director of Broadband Services. We opened a new office in Farmers Branch and brought all dispatchers under one roof. For the first time, I had a private office.

Behind me, I hung a painting of Emperor Tewodros II of Ethiopia, my role model. He had risen from five followers to command an army of 150,000, modernized Ethiopia, and united the nation during the Era of the Princes.

That was the example I sought to follow. Where dispatch had once been scattered with video here, internet there, voice somewhere else, and I united them into one system. Now, any technician can call for support on any product without being bounced around.

It was my own version of what Tewodros had done for Ethiopia: taking divided fiefs and forging them into one.

Closing Reflection

By the time I hung the Tewodros' portrait, I knew I had reached a new chapter in my life. From the boy who once fled Ethiopia with nothing but fear in his heart to the man leading hundreds in one of America's fastest-growing industries, the journey had come full circle.

Tewodros had ended the age of divided princes and united Ethiopia into one nation. In my own way, I had done the same, taking scattered dispatch groups and forging them into one seamless operation. His story reminded me that leadership is not about holding power but about uniting people with a shared purpose.

I had climbed every rung, from installer to director. I had worked through heat, crawled in attics, and had splinters in my skin, insulation in my lungs, through exile and hunger, through setbacks and doubt. And now, with stability, respect, and authority, I felt the satisfaction of having truly built both a career and a life.

The mountain I had once looked up to was now beneath my feet. Yet, I knew: every summit carries with it the winds of change, and the journey of leadership never truly ends.

Part IV: Aiming Higher and Setbacks

Chapter 10 – The Internet Age and Beyond

The mountain I had climbed in Dallas once felt solid beneath my feet, but over time, the winds of change began to blow again. What had once been a place of opportunity slowly turned into a battle of agendas and politics, where performance mattered less than power.

Leading Through Union Renewal

After integrating the dispatch operations, I was given another challenge: overseeing the network dispatchers in Dallas. Unlike other groups, they were unionized, with contracts up for renewal every three years.

HR wanted me to deliver a simple message: tell them to vote for the company. I chose a different approach.

On the final day of the campaign, I stood before the team.

"I was once a frontline employee like you," I told them. "No one ever spoke for me for a fee. I stood on my own and paved my own path. If I can do it, so can you. Vote. It doesn't matter to me who you vote for, but it matters that you vote your conscience."

The union steward, William, who had once worked for me years earlier in Converter Control, interrupted. "You don't have to vote!"

I turned back to the room. "There you have it. The union doesn't want to hear your voice. They only need a handful of votes. I want every one of you to vote your conscience. I rest my case."

When the ballots were counted, 72% chose the company. As employees left the room, I received more handshakes and hugs than after any meeting in my career. That day, I learned something significant: people follow courage, not commands.

A Target on My Back

Despite my results, politics grew sharper. A familiar face returned: the same executive I had once approached in the past with excitement when TCI launched high-speed internet in California. Back then, I had run to his office with a newspaper clipping, eager to share the future. He had dismissed it as irrelevant.

Now, a decade later, he returned as Vice President of Technical Operations. He offered no introductions, no vision, no acknowledgment of what had been built in his absence.

Soon after, a man named Lyle became my direct supervisor. Within weeks, he handed me a poor performance review, though he barely knew my work.

Then, one afternoon, the VP and Lyle appeared in my office unannounced. They paced the floor like vultures circling prey. Finally, the VP said:

"We have a new role for you. We want you to manage the contractors as a manager."

"As a manager?" I asked. "That's a step down."

"You won't lose money," Lyle replied. "So why does it matter?"

"It matters because I didn't earn my position through shortcuts," I replied. "I won't accept a demotion."

Lyle mumbled something that sounded like a warning that refusing would only make things worse. My anger rose. "Do what you must," I said. "You have the right to reassign me, but I have the right not to accept less than I've earned."

They left, but the VP later called again to persuade me. My answer didn't change.

Speaking Out

That weekend was the Company's Volunteering Day, when leaders were expected to attend with their families. Instead, I stayed home and wrote a four-page letter to the head of the company.

I outlined my journey through the ranks, the contributions I had made, and the respect I had earned. "I will not participate in what is called a Cares Day," I wrote, "until I know what the company really cares about."

I explained that I could not, in good faith, bring my children to an event celebrating integrity while I felt betrayed. I ended with words that may have unsettled them: "Whatever happens from here, you cannot deny that you did not know about it."

Days later, the head of HR came to see me. The same executive who had witnessed my leadership during the union vote. When I asked if it was about my letter, he denied it, though we both knew the truth.

"What do you want?" he asked.

I gave him three conditions:

1. Lyle could no longer be my supervisor. He had not earned that position.

2. My review had to be rewritten. Lyle barely knew my work. I even secured a proper review from a previous boss covering ten months of my leadership as backup.

3. My title could not change. I had earned the rank of Director.

All three demands were granted. Lane became my supervisor, and we met at Razzoo's Cajun Café to finalize the review. I joked, "My job has gotten spicy." But deep down, I knew the truth: I was no longer in a place of trust. I was in a snake pit.

Breaking the Glass Ceiling

People often asked me, "Zinah, you've always been in Texas. Have you ever thought about moving somewhere else?"

My answer was always the same: I'll move when I can no longer grow here.

By the mid-2000s, I had reached that point. Time Warner was preparing to acquire the Dallas market, and the same VP who had dismissed me years earlier returned with an offer: "If you stay ninety days after the takeover, you'll get $25,000."

It was a golden handcuff, and I recognized it immediately. My past would be erased, my future discounted.

So, I reached out to Anthony Hayes. "I'm available," I told him. "And I'm done with Texas."

Four years after we had parted ways, Anthony Hayes offered me a new opportunity: Director of Customer Care in Connecticut.

Before I left, Lane and I exchanged gifts at a meeting. He handed me a framed picture of an eagle with the words:

"LEADERSHIP Until you spread your wings, you'll have no idea how far you can fly."

I gave him a silver coin engraved with the image of Emperor Menelik II, the Ethiopian king who, in 1896, led his army to victory at Adwa. That victory sealed forever the truth that Black people are no less and no more than anyone else. Simply equal.

Carrying that pride in my heart, I left Texas to spread my own wings as far north as Connecticut.

On January 15, 2006, I loaded up my Toyota Land Cruiser with my brother-in-law, Tesfa. We drove 1,802 miles across seven states, blaring Ethiopian music and enjoying America the Beautiful. When we reached Connecticut, the ground was blanketed in snow. I had never seen so much of it. It looked like a clean slate.

The day after Martin Luther King Jr. Day, I walked into the Berlin office whispering, "I am free at last." On January 17, I started a new life.

A New Beginning in Connecticut

In Connecticut, I found exactly what I had been seeking: room to grow.

From the start, I excelled as Director of Customer Care. I implemented best practices and used my technical background to support employees who had long felt isolated. For years, Customer Care and Technical Operations had worked at odds, blaming each other. I reminded them we shared one mission: serving the customer.

The results were immediate. Within months, we achieved the highest phone product sales in the region. My leadership was recognized, and soon after, I was promoted to Vice President of Customer Care.

It was proof that leaving Texas had been the right choice. Breaking the glass ceiling had carried me into a new horizon where my skills and experience were not just tolerated. They were celebrated.

Reflection

Texas had been both the foundation of my career and the cage that nearly stifled it. I rose from installer to director there, but I had also faced betrayal, politics, and ceilings that refused to break.

When I finally broke the glass ceiling, I learned something else: the shards can cut you.

Away from the shards and away from the snakes, I went north, as far as I could go.

Connecticut gave me a fresh start. For the first time, I was free to lead without the shadow of old grudges. I had crossed into executive leadership, stepping into a role that once felt unreachable.

The journey had taken me far from the frightened boy who once carried a ladder in a Chevette. Now I stood as a Vice President, responsible for people, products, and customers across a new market.

It was not the end of my climb, but it was proof that no ceiling, no setback, and no snake pit could stop me from rising.

Chapter 11 – Setbacks and Second Chances

In Connecticut, the team struggled at first. The Division President and the Area VP, Anthony Hayes, wanted better performance but not at the expense of morale. His vision was clear: build a team that was not only productive but also proud of its work,

I spent my days walking the floor, answering questions, and working shoulder to shoulder with managers and supervisors. I asked them what it would take for the team to sell the digital voice product, a key part of the product package of TV, internet, and phone strategy.

Gradually, things changed. Energy replaced hesitation. The team's confidence grew, and soon, sales surged. Our results were so strong that I was invited to headquarters to share the best practices we had developed.

Relationships with other departments grew stronger, too, especially with Technical Operations. I worked closely with my peers, and together we made the operation stronger.

But change was constant. Soon, an announcement was made that Anthony Hayes was returning to Texas. He would take over in Houston, leading a market that had transitioned from Time Warner in an exchange between the two companies. Others were going with him. And after only 15 months in Connecticut, I was asked to go too.

In March 2007, I arrived in Houston, back in the state where my American journey had first begun.

In 2008 my father came to visit us in Houston. He was able to witness the life and the family I built after surviving the dark days as a teenager.

A Coin Between Us

Three years later, in 2010, Anthony Hayes posted a job opening for Vice President of Construction. As part of the process, applicants had to interview not only with Anthony but also with their potential peers. On my schedule was Lane, the same man who had once tried to pressure me into stepping down in Dallas.

He arrived on time, smiling at the doorway. "Zinah, are you going in my way?" he asked.

I replied, "Lane, I never wished to get in your way. All I ever wanted was for you not to get in mine. Please, take a seat and let us talk."

As he sat down, Lane pulled a shining silver coin from his pocket. I remembered instantly it was the one I had given him years earlier, bearing the effigy of Emperor Menelik II. He held it out toward me.

"Do you want it back?" he asked.

I shook my head. "No. It was a gift. I can't take it back."

He must have carried it as a good-luck charm all those years. But in the end, the good luck was mine. I was disrespected, but that motivated me to progress in my career.

A Sudden Fall

A few months later, everything shifted. Anthony Hayes left the company. So did others. Reasons were never explained, but everyone knew politics were at play.

Anthony Hayes's replacement quickly targeted me. Perhaps he was insecure, or perhaps it was because I had asked openly why Anthony Hayes couldn't come back. Whatever the reason, in February 2011, I was let go. No explanation was offered.

After years of climbing, I found myself once again outside the gates.

Returning Home

I returned to Ethiopia for two months. In the past, my visits had been brief, two or three weeks at most. This time, I slowed down. I stayed long enough to reconnect with siblings and relatives I had barely known as adults.

We talked late into the night, reliving the past and imagining the future. For the first time, I wasn't visiting as a guest. I was coming home as a man at peace with his journey.

That visit reminded me that life's worth is measured not by the titles we hold but by the connections we nurture and the legacy we build.

Searching for the Next Horizon

When I returned to the United States, I searched for work. In April 2012, I accepted a job with a solar company in Arizona. I hoped solar would follow the same trajectory of growth that cable TV once had. But after a year, the promise dimmed.

So, I began preparing to open my own course. I signed with a franchise operation, identified an automotive shop to buy and convert, and even secured $973,000 in SBA loan.

Then, the phone rang.

It was Anthony Hayes. The company had launched a new product for home security, but it needed to accelerate. "Zinah," he said, "I need you back."

The new role of Senior Director was technically a step down. But sometimes you take one step back to take two forward. I accepted.

I left Houston, stopping along the way to see family and friends. After 2,900 miles on the road, I arrived in Chelmsford, Massachusetts, ready to begin my second round at Comcast. We later settled in Nashua, New Hampshire, and it was quite the contrast from the hot and humid climate in Houston and the dusty, arid Arizona, where I lived for over a year. Now I am in the farthest northern part of the US, where the winter is harsh.

Shoveling snow that was more than six feet high. New Hampshire was a beautiful state.

The Philadelphia Cleanup

No sooner had I settled than Anthony Hayes called again. This time, the challenge was Philadelphia. The company's relationship with the authorities was under pressure. The local government demanded miles of abandoned or tangled cable be removed, or the franchise agreement itself could be at risk.

Anthony Hayes knew if anyone could do the job, it would be me.

One Monday morning, I woke up at 3:00 AM to meet him at the airport. By 5:00 AM, we were on a flight to Philadelphia. At headquarters, the project was outlined, and I was introduced as the man who would get it done.

From that day forward, my weeks had a rhythm. Early Monday mornings, I boarded the first flight to Philadelphia, often turning on the lights in the office long before the local staff arrived. For three days, I oversaw crews in the field, walking neighborhoods, inspecting work, and ensuring accountability. By Wednesday night, I returned home, often arriving in the early hours, only to show up at the division office at 7:30 AM the next morning like everyone else.

Anthony Hayes was an early riser himself, in the office by 6:00 AM and often working late into the night. A year into the project, one morning, he boarded the same 5:00 AM flight to Philadelphia and spotted me already in my seat. "Have you been on this flight since last year?" he asked.

"Yes, sir," I replied. "Every week."

He smiled. He used to call me unrelenting, and that was exactly what I was.

What was supposed to be a six-month cleanup stretched to more than two years. The budget grew, and at its peak, I managed over 200 contractors from four different companies. Each quarter, the city conducted audits. When we failed one, I walked every block of the project myself.

My leadership style was simple: I set the example. The first time I inspected the contractors' work, I was shocked at the trash they left behind: wire clippings, plastic wrapping, and connectors scattered on the ground. I bent down, gathered it all, and walked over to the project manager. I opened his pocket and dropped the trash inside.

Then I told him a story:

"Two inmates, Richard and David, escaped a maximum-security prison. After twenty days on the run, they were caught because of a Pop-Tarts wrapper they left behind. Don't let me find you. Keep your trash where it belongs, on your trucks. No matter how the neighborhood looks, we must leave it better than we found it. Remember, we are here to correct NEC violations and clean up abandoned wires, not create new problems."

I never had to repeat the lesson.

Some days, the decay left endless. From miles away, you could see Comcast's gleaming headquarters rising over a tangled web of abandoned lines sagging across the streets. It was a symbol of the neglect we were fighting to correct.

Not everyone appreciated my style. Once, a local manager sent an email criticizing the contractors' work. I told him my response would be delivered in person. When I showed up at the site, he brought along one of his supervisors, as if he needed backup. I reminded him that the cable plant had been decaying for thirty years because too many leaders sat cocooned in their offices. I was traveling out of state every week, arriving before dawn, working alongside the crews, and he had the nerve to email me from behind his desk. He got the message.

Some parts of Philadelphia were worse than anything I had seen, even in Ethiopia, Sudan, or Kenya. I walked streets littered with spent bullet cartridges. I saw boarded-up houses infested with raccoons, dead cats lying in alleys. One afternoon, I turned on the news and saw that three bodies had been pulled from a garage on the very block where I had walked just days earlier, supervising crews.

Every Wednesday night, when I came home, my quiet neighborhood felt like a resort.

At about the halfway mark, my former colleague joined me. He was focused, meticulous, curious, and unrelenting, qualities that made him the perfect fit for such a mission. His dedication and straightforward personality steadied the effort and carried it forward.

Six months before the end of the project, another assignment came my way. By then, my replacement had fully taken the driver's seat. I told him, "You can always call me with questions," and a couple of times, I still joined him on city audits. But the day-to-day responsibility was his.

With the Philadelphia cleanup nearing completion, Anthony Hayes turned to me with a new challenge: Maryland.

Reflection

This chapter of my life proved that careers are never straight lines. I had risen, fallen, and risen again. I had been dismissed without cause, yet returned stronger. I had seen the darkest neighborhoods of Philadelphia and walked among the worst neglect, but I had also seen what persistence, accountability, and unrelenting discipline could achieve.

The lesson was simple: setbacks are not endings. They are turning points.

Every time I was tested, I found a way forward. And now, with Philadelphia behind me, a new challenge waited in Maryland.

The Maryland Assignment

When the Philadelphia cleanup finally began to taper, Anthony Hayes pulled me aside about a new temporary assignment in Maryland. Not long after, I also received a call from the Senior Vice President. It was explained that the Area Vice President of the region was "retiring," and they needed me to step in for about six months until a permanent replacement could be found.

Six months? I smiled at the number, but in my head, I translated it into dog months. The Philadelphia project had also been scoped for six months, and it stretched into almost three years. That was the difference between boardroom estimates and field reality. From the ivory tower, executives calculated best-case scenarios, but three miles from their offices, NEC violations dangled from most cable lines.

Understanding the Structure

The company spanned many states and organized into three divisions, I belonged to the one of the divisions. Within the division were five regions, each headed by a leader.

Philadelphia had been a special assignment, outside the normal hierarchy. Now, my focus has shifted to one of the regions. The region's plant stretched an estimated 24,000 miles of cable, not including house drops. That was enough to circle the Earth three times. My temporary role was to serve as the acting Vice President for one-third of the region, roughly one trip around the globe in cable.

About 800 employees worked across multiple fulfillment centers. Center Managers reported to Directors. Directors reported to the VP. For the next several months, that VP was me.

Taking the Role to Heart

Titles never moved me. Outcomes did. I took the role as seriously as any permanent post. A story I'd heard as a boy guided me: a man on death row racing to finish an invention in his final days, not for applause, but for his conscience. That ethic stayed with me. Do the work because it must be done.

So, I worked as if 2011 had never happened. I held no grudge against the company, even after being pushed out. After all, The company had given me years of paychecks in return for work I believed in. Now I would serve the team in front of me, and the leaders I respected, Anthony Hayes and his boss, Kevin, with the same intensity as ever.

Living the Assignment

I came to Maryland and went to the office every day, just like those who lived a few miles away, even though I commuted from New Hampshire. I was told I could work from home on Fridays, but my conscience wouldn't allow it. Instead, I worked a full day on Fridays and flew home afterward. Many Saturdays, I arrive home at 1:00 AM.

I often ate my meals in airports. I answered emails in terminal seats, reviewed reports, and carried the work with me wherever I went. I gave it everything I had.

In my head, the words of Kool Moe Dee's rap rang: "I go to work... like a doctor." And that was exactly what I did, I was going to work like the AVP I had been asked to be.

Turning Around a Struggling Region

The area I stepped into had the lowest performance in the region. Employee morale was poor, and some leaders were disengaged. One manager even told me, "You'll leave soon, just like the others, and things will continue as they were."

I looked him in the eye and said, "That's the wrong thinking. I am not like the others. I am the cheetah - swift, calculating, and unwilling to let go until the job is done."

Not long after, Jasper was named our Regional VP of Technical Operations. He reported to Mary, and I reported to him. Jasper was full of energy, open-minded, respectful, and diplomatic. Most importantly, he believed in straightforward feedback given at the right time and in the right place. He often quoted Proverbs 27:17: "As iron sharpens iron, so one man sharpens another."

That resonated deeply with me. Jasper created the environment for me to do my best work.

Someone told Jasper, "Z doesn't work like a temporary." He shared the comment with me, watching my reaction. I told him, "Nothing is permanent. I remember when companies changed the phrase from 'permanent employee' to 'full-time employee.' We don't even know if we'll be alive tomorrow. The only thing we can do is give our best today, because this day will never come again."

Becoming Permanent

Weeks became months, and I was asked if I wanted to apply for the permanent AVP role.

I applied, and the interview felt more like a formality. Everyone had already witnessed my commitment.

Jasper asked me during the interview, "What if we don't pick you?"

"I'll be disappointed if you choose me over someone more qualified," I said. "I want the right person in the right seat for the best outcome. I only want to be where I'm wanted, and I never want to be the guest who overstayed his welcome."

In May 2017, I was officially offered the role. We sold our home in New Hampshire, and by August 2017, we had settled in Maryland.

Reflection

Maryland was more than just another assignment. It was proof that I could step into a struggling environment, rally a team, and rebuild morale while driving performance. It was there that I learned that leadership is not about permanence. It's about presence. Each day is a chance to lead as if it were your last.

I came in as a temporary, but I left as the Area Vice President. The cheetah had run his course, swift and unrelenting, and claimed new ground.

Chapter 12 – The Descent

My area of responsibility stretched across Delaware, most of Maryland, and a sliver of West Virginia. Taylor managed DC and a smaller portion of Maryland, while Carter covered Virginia with its vast geography.

Taylor was sharp, decisive, and demanding. He used to joke about "burgs and vills," since nearly every town in his district ended with one of those endings. But behind the humor was a man who prescribed only one day's worth of medicine for a ten-day illness. Some employees recovered under him. Others didn't survive the pace.

If Taylor had been a doctor, he would have prescribed a single day's worth of medicine. Some patients would recover, but some wouldn't survive.

If I were the doctor, I would give you ten days. My approach was different: time, space, and room for people to succeed.

Carter was wise, calm, organized, and meticulous, with flawless follow-up. He brought steadiness where others brought fire.

Reshaping the Region

We spent long days in strategy sessions, working to reconfigure the 40 geographic areas of the region and determine how many managers were needed to run them. The conversations were candid, creative, and often sharp.

At one point, Jasper, our Regional VP, looked around the room and said, "Do some people realize what this means? If it comes down to it and their jobs are on the line, would they still give the same input?"

He was right. In some ways, we were sharpening the very knife that could cut us. But I had lived through worse. I remembered Sudan. I don't stop the train. I either get out of the way or I ride it.

In 2019, the three areas were consolidated into two. Taylor took on the new carved-out territory. Carter and I survived. James, a newer addition, was cut.

Jasper moved on, and one of our peers took his place. More consolidation followed, this time with me in the crosshairs. Three of us were told to apply for a Senior Director role, essentially a demotion.

Refusing to Step Down

I was asked for my decision. Option one: leave. Option two: apply for a step down.

I said neither.

I wouldn't leave willingly, and I would not apply for a lesser role. It smelled like 2011 all over again, but this time it was handled with civility, transparency, and open discussion the right way.

I reached out for help to see if there were other options. I laid out my options. He already knew, but Anthony Hayes was by the book. He would not interfere. The initiative had to come from me.

There were jobs to choose from. I selected Division Vice President of Workforce Operations, overseeing 600 employees, two Directors, dozens of managers, and more than 50 supervisors. It was a massive responsibility, but one that I embraced.

The Final Stretch

Then came the pandemic. COVID-19 swept across the world, and overnight, offices emptied. Managing teams suddenly meant managing homes, screens, and uncertainty. Communication shifted, and leadership required empathy more than ever before.

Anthony Hayes eventually moved on to another division.

In September 2022, I was on a call with my boss and the VP of HR. The news came bluntly: I could leave in two weeks or stay until the end of the year. My department would be combined under another VP, and one of my direct reports would fill any gaps.

I pushed back. More time was better not just for me, but for the company. I presented a list of things I could do to help with the transition. They hesitated.

Then I asked about others who had "retired," but stayed for six months or even a year. Why not me?

Eventually, they agreed. My official end date was set for March 2023.

Sunset

I had known this day would come. Ever since 2011, I had lived like a man who kept a loaded gun under his pillow, not out of bitterness, but readiness.

When the end finally arrived, I accepted it with dignity. I left The company after nearly four decades in the industry.

I went to Europe with my family, not in mourning but in celebration of survival, of resilience, of the long climb that had begun with a ladder stuffed into a Chevette.

I had ridden the train as far as it would take me. At last, I stepped off and into the sunset.

My career had taken me from poles and attics to boardrooms and strategy sessions. I had been tested by splinters, sweat, betrayal, and politics. I survived restructurings, demotions, and dismissals. I had risen to lead teams across states, thousands of employees, and millions of customers.

In the end, the titles mattered less than the journey. What mattered was the work, the people, and the values I carried with me: courage, dignity, and resilience.

I left not as a man defeated, but as one who had given his all. My career did not end with a fall, but with a landing.

Final Approach

Every flight has its turbulence, its climbs, its descent. My career was like that, a long journey across continents, storms, and skies that sometimes felt endless. But eventually, every journey turns toward its final approach.

For me, that landing meant returning to the foundation that had always carried me: faith, family, education, and identity. They were the compass points that guided me from the refugee camps of Sudan to the boardrooms of America.

The engines had quieted, but the journey, the real one, continued.

Part V: Aiming Higher and Setbacks

Chapter 13 – Foundations of a New Life

Citizenship by Choice

Marriage, family, and career would come in time, but one step I knew I had to take first was securing my place in the country that had given me refuge. After nine years in America, I applied for U.S. citizenship.

The decision was both practical and deeply emotional. One day, Enana and I called the Ethiopian Embassy in Washington, D.C. The staff were rude, short-tempered, and dismissive. A man named Negash put us on hold, then disappeared for so long that someone else picked up the line and casually said, "He went to lunch."

That moment crystallized something for me: in Ethiopia, I had grown up in a system where citizens were treated as guilty until proven innocent, where governments could kill without hesitation, and where those in exile were treated like burdens instead of sons. In Sudan, I had been an unwelcome guest, subject to raids and jail. In Kenya, I was denied from working during the best years of my youth. But in the U.S., I had been received without condition.

A church had paid for my airfare. Catholic Charities had handed me $150 and wished me luck. No one demanded anything in return. America gave me not only shelter but dignity. Yes, racism existed and yes hypocrisy too. But for me, America was and still is the best.

I became a U.S. citizen in 1991. To this day, when people ask if I am American, I answer: "Yes by choice, not just by birth." The holiday I celebrate most passionately is July 4. I know in my bones the meaning of "the land of the free, home of the brave."

Building a Family

Marriage was always on my mind, but my life didn't follow the usual American sequence of college, career, and then family. Mine was a life built on the go, more like a mechanic fixing a moving car than someone cruising on a smooth road.

Most of us Ethiopians who had settled in America were young men in our early twenties. Women were few, and those who were here were quickly spoken for. My relative Tsehay, who lived in New York, sometimes introduced me to people she trusted. One day, she gave me a name and number but added, "Please don't do anything that comes back to me. I'm close with her brothers."

That was how I first connected with Enana, who was living in New York at the time but visiting Dallas for a few days. She was polite but hesitant. I called, she avoided, and then slowly we began to talk. On one of her visits to Dallas, after many conversations, she agreed to meet me outside her workplace. I was thirty-five miles away, but I didn't want to lose the chance.

We spoke briefly in the parking lot, and I asked if we could sit for coffee. At the café, as the waitress handed us menus, I realized I didn't have enough cash for more than two coffees. Nervous, I warned her against ordering dessert, joking that too much cake would ruin her teeth in America, where dentists were everywhere. She believed me, and I was saved from embarrassment.

Later, on a proper date at Reunion Arena's revolving restaurant, she ordered cheesecake. I laughed inside so much at my story about sweets, and I joined her. That night, we truly began to fall in love.

I wanted her to see my real life, so I took her to the trailer park where I lived. "This is where poor people live who can't afford houses," I told her. She asked, "Is it yours?" I said yes. She replied, "That's all that matters." In that moment, I knew she was the one.

We married soon after, surrounded by friends. Jefri, Demelash, and Teshome stood with me as groomsmen; Mimi, Meklit, Abir, and Alem were her bridesmaids. Zena sang, Addisu took photos, and our community celebrated with us.

Together, we built a modest life. We both worked and studied, saving $17,000. With help from Enana's nephew, Asefa, we bought our first home near Eastfield College: a 919-square-foot, three-bedroom, one-bath house for $23,500. Some laughed, "They call this a house?" But four years later, when we built a new two-story brick house and moved in, those same people said, "With patience, butter comes from milk."

By then, Mahlet had been born, filling our home with joy. Soon after, Markos arrived, and our family felt complete.

Our family portrait.

Education Without End

Just as family life took shape, I continued to pursue education in every form I could find. For me, learning was never a straight line. I learned early that real education came not only from classrooms but from life itself.

What good is it to have a degree and not a job for which I went to school? In my English 102 class, the instructor told us she had a PhD and was getting an annual salary of $25,000 but at that same time, I was already earning $1,000 more than her. I wanted my work and my education to be complementary.

Within months of my arrival in Dallas, I enrolled at Richland College. It became a safe space to ask questions, even about words I heard for the first time. I bought the best dictionary I could find. I took classes in reading, writing, and comprehension. I welcomed corrections whenever someone noticed my accent. Speech classes forced me to stand and talk before others.

When I later studied Radio/TV at East Texas University, I even worked as a radio DJ reading weather reports and news while my professors criticized every word. At Richland, I once wrote a paper titled Ragtime. My instructor was stunned. "How long have you been in this country?" he asked. "A year," I replied. He shook his head. "If I were in his country, I'd be homeless."

I bought self-study programs like Verbal Advantage, listened to talk shows instead of music, and even watched children's TV programs, knowing I had missed the cultural references that American kids grew up with. On weekends, I watched Westerns like Gunsmoke and The Rifleman. Those shows were always about good and evil, about men carrying guns but trying to resolve conflicts without using them. They reminded me of my father's dignity in Ethiopia, and I related deeply to their lessons. At the same time, their dialogue sharpened my English and gave me another window into American culture.

Once my English was stronger, I pursued formal studies. In 1989, I earned an Associate's degree in General Studies. I came within a semester of a bachelor's degree at East Texas Sate University, but changed course when my career pulled me elsewhere. In 1998, I earned an Applied Science degree in Digital Electronics from Eastfield College. By 2000, I had completed a bachelor's in business administration from Amberton University, balancing classes with my first supervisory role in cable.

Over the years, I pursued executive training at Harvard and UCLA. In 2021, after retiring, I returned once more to school through SNHU's online program. In February 2024, I earned my MBA with a specialization in Consulting.

That final degree felt like more than just a credential. It was a golden opportunity to bring together everything I had lived, learned, and led to turn my experiences into lessons for others. This memoir itself is part of that mission: my consulting project for life, a way to tell an untold story for my family, for others, and for generations to come. In the two years of my MBA, I wrote so many papers, it gave me confidence that I can really pull off a book writing project on my own. Here we are.

Reflection

By the early 1990s, I had a citizenship I chose, a family I cherished, and an education I built piece by piece. None of it came in straight lines or easy steps.

I came to this country with ten dollars in my pocket and broken English. I built a family out of love, not wealth. I built a career out of determination, not privilege. And I built my education from every corner I could, from classrooms, radios, dictionaries, talk shows, Western movies, and hard work.

America was not perfect. But it gave me the freedom to be imperfect and still move forward. With Enana by my side, my children at my feet, and a story finally written down, I had laid the true foundation of my life.

Family and Community

Family does not arrive in neat packages, but it comes in siblings, cousins, nephews, nieces, friends, and communities that slowly become as close as blood. My journey in America was never solitary. Alongside my wife and children, I was lifted, supported, and enriched by family ties that spanned oceans and generations.

Arrival of Siblings

In 1999, my younger sister Sefrash arrived in the U.S. with her son Bisrat, only ninety days old. She settled with us in Dallas. His father was unable to come, and I didn't want Bisrat to grow up without a father figure. I let him call me daddy. When my sister was away, he often stayed with me. Many evenings, I rushed out of work unfinished just to pick him up from daycare by 6:00 PM. There was no VPN or remote work then, where I would sometimes show up at the Richardson office at 3:00 AM, work for a few hours, take a nap at home, and then return by 7:00 AM as if I had just arrived fresh. Few knew of those sacrifices.

In 2003, my older brother arrived and settled in Maryland. He visited us in Texas a couple of years later, and that's when we decided it was time to tell Bisrat the truth about his father. We gathered around a table and placed a photo of his father in front of him. "This is your father," we said. Bisrat looked puzzled, then at me. I nodded, confirming it. We pointed at my brother and said, "This is your uncle." Then he turned back to me. After a pause, he said, "That is my uncle daddy." It was the greatest compliment I could ever receive, to be acknowledged as both an uncle and a father figure. Today, Bisrat is grown, a professional, and he still calls me pops.

My younger brother also came, eventually settling in Georgia with his wife. Together, they raised five children.

Enana's Side of the Family

Enana's family also built strong roots in America. Her nephew came early, around the same time I did, and helped pave the way for many, including Enana herself. Asefa has been by our side since the day we met. He helped us purchase our first home and was present for so many important milestones.

Over the years, Enana's extended family spread across Dallas, Chicago, and Washington, while the earliest arrivals built a base in New York.

A Journey Across America

In the summer of 2003, I decided it was time to show my children their country not just through textbooks or TV, but with their own eyes. America the Beautiful had given me so much, and I wanted them to see it, to touch it, to feel proud of the land they called home.

Mahlet was twelve then, already developing a thoughtful maturity. Markos was eight, full of energy and questions. And little Bisrat was only four, small but determined to keep up with his older siblings. Together, the four of us set out from Dallas, bound westward on a journey that would stretch nearly two weeks and cover more than five thousand miles.

Our adventure had its own rhythm. Each time we arrived in a new town or hotel, we made our entrance in a way that became almost ceremonial: Bisrat leading with his tiny carry-on, Markos behind him, then Mahlet, and finally me bringing up the rear. Marching in single file, in perfect order of age, we must have looked like a little parade, one family determined to experience the vastness of their country together. And just as we entered, we always left the same way, our miniature procession moving out into the unknown.

Our first stop was Albuquerque, New Mexico. The red desert stretched wide, and the air was dry and sharp. From there, we pressed on to the Hoover Dam, where I showed them one of America's greatest feats of engineering, built during the Great Depression, a reminder of what people could accomplish even in the hardest of times.

In Las Vegas, neon lights dazzled their young eyes, though our purpose there was not gambling but to attend the wedding of Stephanie and Eddie, two coworkers of mine. The children saw a different side of celebration and togetherness. From there, we continued west to Los Angeles, where the children's laughter filled Universal Studios, and then to Hermosa Beach, where they splashed into the Pacific Ocean for the first time. I watched them play in the waves, and it struck me that I was giving them something I had never known as a child: the chance to see and explore a world beyond their own doorstep.

Turning eastward again, we crossed into Arizona, stopping in Phoenix before heading north to Flagstaff to stand at the edge of the Grand Canyon. There, the earth itself seemed to open into eternity. I watched my children peer into that vast chasm, and I knew they were seeing not just nature's grandeur but the measure of human smallness in the face of creation.

Our last major stop was Carlsbad Caverns in Texas, where we descended into the dark, otherworldly depths of the caves. Finally, tired but enriched, we returned home to Dallas. Two weeks of constant travel, countless new sights, and more than 5,000 miles driven, a journey stitched into their childhoods.

For me, it wasn't just a road trip. It was a lesson, a gift. I wanted Mahlet, Markos, and Bisrat to know that this country was theirs, to recognize its beauty, its history, and its possibilities. And I wanted them to see, through our little single-file march into each new place, that wherever we went, we went together, each one with their own path, yet part of the same line.

Reflection

When I first arrived in America, I had only ten dollars in my pocket and broken English on my tongue. I learned about this country step by step, one bus ride, one rented room, one unfamiliar street at a time. Now, decades later, I was the father leading three children across thousands of miles of highways, showing them the land that had once been a mystery to me.

The road trip was not only about America's wonders, the Hoover Dam, the Grand Canyon and the Pacific Ocean but also about passing on a sense of belonging. I wanted them to know that this nation was not just where they were born but where their father had fought to plant roots, where their mother had sacrificed, and where their family could grow. In giving them America, I was also giving them a piece of myself: the journey from a refugee to a man proud to call this place home.

Santa's Secret

One Christmas Eve, Enana had an idea to make the holiday extra special for Mahlet and Markos. I owned a Santa suit, complete with a fake beard and hat, and decided to play the part myself. In the garage, I put on the costume, slipped out through the back driveway, circled around, and knocked on the front door.

When they answered, I boomed, "Ho, ho, ho! Merry Christmas, Mahlet and Markos!" They were three and seven years old at the time, and their eyes widened with shock. Santa knew their names! They squealed with excitement, grabbed me by the hand, and begged me to come inside.

I sat down on the sofa, enjoying the moment of pure joy on their faces. But then Mahlet's sharp eyes caught something. She looked down at my shoes and said with certainty, "Those are Dadi's shoes!"

The game was up. I pulled down the beard and admitted the truth about Santa was that their father is Santa. Their smiles fell, replaced with the first twinges of disappointment that every child eventually feels when fantasy collides with reality.

That night, I told them the real magic of Christmas wasn't in a man from the North Pole, but in the love of family and in mothers and fathers who bring joy into their children's lives.

Reflection

Even though the secret didn't last long, the lesson stayed with me. The joy we create for our children doesn't have to come from myths or costumes. It comes from being present, sharing in their laughter, and building memories they will carry long after the magic of Santa fades.

Friends Who Became Family

Not all families come by blood, but some are chosen along the way. One summer, we rented a van and drove from Dallas through Louisiana to

Daytona Beach, Florida, then up the winding roads of the Smoky Mountains into Gatlinburg, Tennessee. We continued north to Boston to show our children Harvard and MIT, planting seeds of aspiration, and then to Washington, D.C., to see Capitol Hill and the White House. By the time we returned to Texas, we had driven over 5,000 miles. The rental agent stared in disbelief at the odometer, asking how we could possibly have covered that much ground in just ten days. For us, it was proof of the joy of shared journeys.

Other friends wove themselves into our story. Neighbors who helped care for our kids when they were small. People whom I had known since Kenya, and later, he joined me at the Dallas Times Herald. My neighbor Teshome became like a brother. When I had a mobile home, I convinced him to move in with me to save money on rent, under one condition: he too had to buy a gun for safety. We both carried our .357 Magnums and even practiced at the shooting range before he later moved to Oklahoma for school. He is settled, married to Meseret and has raised his children into adults.

There was also a friend who came to us through my childhood friend. He lived with us for a while before moving on to settle his own life.

In Houston, we connected with more friends: Each family added to the strength of our community, celebrating birthdays, graduations, and milestones together.

Anchors of Support

Community ties became anchors in every city we lived in. In Connecticut, we found comfort in neighbors, who became extended family. In Dallas, we leaned on those who were among the earliest arrivals in our Ethiopian family. In Houston, Enana reunited with her childhood friend, and together with their families, they shared countless memories.

Even in small encounters, the strength of the community shone through. When Mahlet was born, Enana's hospital room overflowed with flowers from friends. The woman in the next bed had none, and we shared ours to bring her comfort. Years later, when a man in Dallas fell ill, he received so many visitors that hospital staff wondered aloud if he was royalty. That is the way our community loves and shows up in numbers, in presence, and in spirit.

Continuing the Bond Across Generations

From our parents who knew each other in Ethiopia, to our generation, and now to our children's generation, the bond continues unbroken. It is one of the reasons I felt compelled to write this book, to ensure that these stories, our stories, are memorialized for the generations yet to come.

Reflection

Looking back, I see how much of my strength came not only from my own will but from the people around me. Family by blood, family by marriage, and family by choice and each played a role in my journey. From Dallas to Connecticut to Houston, the Ethiopian community offered me comfort, and solidarity.

We are few, but we coalesce like no other. We celebrate together, mourn together, and raise our children together. And in that unity, I found roots as strong as any I had left behind in Ethiopia.

Chapter 14 – Lifting Others

Throughout my journey, I have been lifted by many families, friends, coworkers, and mentors. In turn, I made it my responsibility to lift others, both inside and outside the workplace. Leadership, I came to believe, was not about climbing alone but about pulling others up the ladder with you.

Mentoring in the Workplace

When I first became a supervisor, my bosses handed me a stack of resumes for open positions. One candidate was quickly dismissed. They called him a "job hopper" and doubted his commitment. Something inside me pushed back. I saw a capable man who simply had not yet found the right place.

I argued for the candidate. I told my leaders that if he failed, I would take responsibility. They agreed reluctantly, but they gave me the chance to hire him. Mulugeta not only did the job well, but he also thrived. He worked for the company for 17 years. My bosses noticed too and not only did he prove them wrong, but I had been willing to take a risk for someone I believed in. That moment taught me something about leadership: people need someone to see them differently than the world does.

There were many others. Derek, a technician who stood out for his discipline and curiosity, caught my attention early. I encouraged him, gave him stretch assignments, and watched as he rose into leadership roles. Another young technician brimmed with energy and intelligence. I promoted him to supervisor, and he went on to become a project manager. In each of them, I saw a reflection of my own early struggles, and I knew how much difference a single "yes" could make.

Not all mentoring moments came from promotions. Sometimes, they came from redirection. In Arizona, when I briefly took on a management role, one employee filled the room with endless "Yo Mama" jokes. Instead of embarrassing her, I asked her to turn it around: "Make them positive jokes," I told her. She laughed and accepted the challenge. Soon, the team was roaring with fun, this time in a way that built people up instead of tearing them down.

For me, mentoring was never about power or authority. It was about creating a space where people could grow, find dignity in their work, and even find joy in it.

From Insult to Shoeshine

When I was working at El Centro Job Training Center, one day my supervisor, Julius and a few coworkers were talking together. I casually shared with the group that Ethiopians had our own cuisine. Julius cut me off with a sneer and said, "What do you guys eat, horse di**?" Then he laughed as if it was funny.

The words were so crude and disrespectful that they did not even deserve a reply. He carried himself as though being a supervisor gave him license to humiliate others, and I silently marked the kind of man he was.

Two decades later, life had taken us both in very different directions. I was at DFW airport, dressed in a suit and tie, preparing to fly to Tucson, Arizona for a job interview with Cox Communications. As I walked past the shoeshine stand, I stopped in my tracks. Standing there, waiting for a customer, was Julius.

I looked again to be sure, then stepped forward and called his name. He recognized me immediately, though the embarrassment on his face showed that he wished I had not.

I asked him straight, "Are you the shoeshine?" He answered quietly, "Yes."

I took a seat, letting him shine my shoes. He hoped I had forgotten the insult years earlier, but I had not. Instead of bringing it up, I asked him how he ended up here, shining shoes at an airport after once holding a supervisor's title. His explanation was vague. He said the work gave him freedom, but it was clear to me what had really happened. Men who use their position to belittle others eventually collapse under the weight of their own flaws.

When he finished, I shared my own journey. I told him that since the days at El Centro, I had pursued a career in the cable television industry, earning several promotions. I told him I had been a supervisor like him, but I had chosen a different path, learning from leaders both good and bad, applying those lessons, and rising through the ranks to become Director of Technical Operations. That day, I was on my way to another interview to further expand my experience.

I paid the fee, added a tip, and wished him good luck.

As I walked away, I thought about the symmetry of the moment. The man who had once disrespected me stood at my feet, literally polishing my shoes. For me, the lesson was clear: poor leaders destroy themselves. True leaders rise not by stepping on others, but by lifting them up.

Reflection

That day at the airport reminded me of a lesson I carried through every stage of my career: leadership is not about power, but about respect. A title may put you above others for a time, but arrogance and cruelty eventually collapse under their own weight. True leadership is measured by how people remember you when the title is gone. Julius had once been my supervisor, but through his own failures, he ended up at my feet. I, on the other hand, had risen not by stepping on others, but by lifting them up.

The Mentors Who Lifted Me

Of course, I could not have lifted others without those who lifted me first.

The Director of Technical Operations was one of the earliest. He believed in me when I made the leap from front-line technical work to supervision. He saw potential where others only saw a risk.

Others came later, and he became both mentor and brother-in-arms. He challenged me to think bigger, to lead larger, and to carry myself with confidence even in hostile environments.

And then there was the Regional Vice President in Maryland. His favorite saying was, "Iron sharpens iron." He believed in honest feedback given at the right time, and he lived it. His diplomacy, energy, and fairness gave me the freedom to do my best. Leaders like Anthony Hayes and Jasper sharpened me. They tested me, encouraged me, and reminded me that leadership is forged in the fire of accountability and trust.

Lifting Communities

Beyond the walls of The company, I also felt a duty to lift the communities I came from.

I served as President of the National Association for Multi-Ethnicity in Communications (NAMIC), an organization dedicated to ensuring diversity and inclusion in the industry. NAMIC gave me a network of peers and mentors, and the chance to mentor younger professionals. I benefited directly from this, attending an executive development program at UCLA, but I gave back by helping others find their path into leadership.

In Houston, I served on the board of Career Recovery Resources, an organization dedicated to helping people whose lives had been disrupted, whether through addiction, incarceration, homelessness, or military service. Their struggles were different from mine, but I could relate. I, too, had known disruption. I, too, had faced closed doors. I wanted to be part of opening new ones for them.

Within the Ethiopian community, I gave my time and skills wherever I could. I wired microphones and speakers for Dallas's first Ethiopian church on Maple Avenue. I helped form the Gojjam Development Association, later expanded into GOSHNA (Gojjam Self-Help Association in North America), which provided childcare for orphans in Ethiopia. I remember one meeting where endless arguments over money left me in tears. To break the deadlock, I asked for a child's name, wrote a check for $180, and said,

"This is not about the amount. It's about the child." The debate stopped, and the support flowed.

In 2016, after the government's massacre of more than 55 peaceful youth in Bahir Dar, we created the Gojjam Global Alliance. I helped lead it. We raised funds, worked long nights, and spoke for the voiceless. Through that effort, we fought for a young man who had fled after his brother was murdered at Axum University. Endalew was detained by U.S. immigration officers, facing a terrifying uncertainty. We rallied the community, raised ~$12,000 through a Crowdfunding platform, hired a lawyer, and secured his release. Today, Endalew is safe and free in America.

These moments mattered deeply to me. My job paid me, but this work nourished me.

Reflection

When I look back, I see a pattern: I was lifted, and I lifted others. My mentors sharpened me, and I sharpened those I was entrusted to lead. Sometimes it was one person, like Mulugeta, who just needed someone to see him differently. Sometimes it was a whole community, struggling in the shadow of violence or neglect.

Leadership, I learned, is not about titles or paychecks. It is about what you leave behind: people's confidence, dignity, opportunity, and sometimes even their freedom.

I came to this country with almost nothing. Along the way, I found people who believed in me. And in return, I gave my belief to others. That cycle of lifting up and down, generation to generation, is what sustained me through every setback and every success.

Chapter 15 – Reflection: A Life Repaired in Motion

I have often said my life was like repairing a moving vehicle while still driving it. Nothing came to me in neat order: education, career, family, or stability. I had to patch, fix, and build as I went along, often with little more than courage and determination. But through resilience, faith, and the support of many, the vehicle kept moving forward.

It was also like my country of birth, Ethiopia with its deep ravines, torrential rains, rivers hiding crocodiles, snakes in the grass, steep valleys, jagged mountains, and a lawless government. Yet amid all of that danger, Ethiopia was still green, breathtakingly beautiful, and filled with the warmth of families and friends. My life has carried both realities at once, the perils that could have swallowed me, and the beauty that nourished me and gave me strength to go on.

Looking back, I see that survival alone was never enough. I wanted more than safety; I wanted dignity, purpose, and the chance to build. Every struggle in the refugee camps, the long nights in Dallas, the battles within corporate boardrooms taught me to keep moving forward, even when the road ahead was uncertain.

I came to this country with $10 in my pocket and broken English. I leave my career with my head held high, my family beside me, and my story written not just in these pages but in the lives, I've touched along the way.

For me, America has become more than a place of refuge. It was the land where my potential could finally be seen. I am proud to say I am an American by choice, not by birthright. This country, imperfect as it is, gave me the room to fight, to grow, and to contribute.

And yet, Ethiopia has never left me. The lessons of my father's dignity, the memories of my mother's sacrifice, and the unbreakable bond of siblings and friends continue to guide me. I stand on both soils, the red earth of my homeland and the wide expanse of my adopted country.

Now, in retirement, I no longer race against deadlines or fight for promotions. I measure success in quieter terms: the laughter of my children, the wisdom I can pass to the next generation.

If my story says anything, it is this: life will never give you perfect roads. Sometimes it is ravines and snakes; sometimes it is highways wide open. But with resilience, with courage, with faith, you can keep moving forward, repairing as you go, building as you live, and always finding beauty in the struggle.

The Passing of My Parents

The first time I returned to Ethiopia was for two reasons. The military junta had finally fallen, and I was free to go back. But the return was not only about freedom. It was also about mourning. During the civil war, my youngest brother had been killed. I went home to grieve with my family, to stand on the soil where their lives had ended too soon.

That visit taught me something: not every trip home had to be in response to tragedy. I resolved then that I would go back often, not just to bury the dead, but to celebrate the living. And I did. I went again and again, making the choice to be present for holidays and family moments, to carry joy instead of only grief.

But loss still found me. On one visit, I arrived to find my mother on her deathbed. I did all I could to extend her time, staying by her side, offering comfort in whatever small ways were left to me. Eight days after I arrived, she passed away. I had the chance to carry her body, to bury her with my own hands, to mourn her as a son should. For a long time, I felt that I could have done more, but family and friends comforted me, saying she had waited for me to return, to say goodbye before she let go.

My father lived longer, reaching the age of eighty-five. Technology kept us connected. With Wubetu's help, we spoke often on video calls. He was very sick near the end, and I wrestled with the question of whether to fly back once more. But it was during the pandemic, and I feared that I might bring him more harm than comfort. I stayed, and later Enana told me he had passed away.

In the end, I went to Ethiopia seven times, of which five were for proactive visits, one to say a final farewell. I was far away, but never too far to be supportive, to give what I could. Now, with my parents gone, I feel the mantle has shifted: I am no longer only a son, I am the second oldest in the family, carrying the weight of memory and responsibility.

My parents left us an oral legacy where stories were told at night, lessons handed down across generations. Our grandparents and great-grandparents did the same. But as the most traveled of my family, and the first to cross Ethiopia's borders in search of freedom, I feel a particular duty. These words, these memories, are my offering: a written legacy, preserved not just for today, but for the generations yet to come.

Author's Note

As I bring this book to completion, I have contemplated the language in which it should be told. I gave the English version priority, knowing that publishing and reaching readers in the United States would be easier in English. Yet, my heart belongs also to Amharic, the language in which many of these memories were first lived, spoken, and remembered.

One day, if this story finds its audience, I hope to write a version in Amharic for those who wish to read it in the rhythm and depth of our mother tongue. My journey is not only mine, but also Ethiopia's, and it feels right to offer it in the words of both homes I have known.

Vignette: The Chevette and the Ladder

It was not a truck. Anyone with eyes could see that. It was a blue 1979 Chevette, small and boxy, hardly the kind of vehicle a cable technician would drive. Yet for me, it was all I had.

When the contracting manager asked to inspect my "truck," my stomach tightened. I had no truck. But I walked with him to the parking lot and pointed anyway.

"That one," I said.

He squinted. "That's a car."

I nodded. "It does the job of a truck."

I opened the trunk. Inside, he saw my climbing gear, toolbox, and power drill neatly arranged. Then I opened the passenger door and showed him how I had removed the front seat so I could slide a six-foot ladder into the car. It fits snug and secure, as if the car had been built for it.

The man laughed, shaking his head. "How did you even get this in here?"

"Carefully," I said. "And I don't need a twenty-eight-foot extension ladder. There isn't a pole in Dallas that I can't climb with my gear. The day you find one, you can fire me."

Something in my voice must have convinced him. He chuckled again, not in mockery but in admiration. "You're hired," he said.

From then on, the Chevette became more than a car. It was a symbol. Customers would open their doors, glance past me, and ask, "Where's your truck?"

I would smile and point back at the little blue car. "That's it," I'd say. "It carries everything I need."

What others saw as a limitation, I treated as an advantage. That car, with its missing passenger seat and overstuffed trunk, was my first company vehicle, my first investment in a career that would span nearly forty years.

Reflection

The Chevette taught me one of life's most important lessons: you don't wait for the perfect conditions to begin. You start with what you have.

To many, it was just an old car. To me, it was a declaration that nothing, not even the lack of a truck, would stop me from stepping into my future.

That little car carried more than tools; it carried determination, creativity, and the belief that solutions matter more than excuses. Looking back, it was never about the vehicle. It was about the drive.

Vignette: Uncle Dadi

When my sister arrived in Dallas in 1999, she brought with her a three-month-old baby boy. His father could not come, and I quietly decided that the boy would never feel the absence. He would have someone to look up to, someone to call Daddy.

I picked him up from daycare many evenings, sometimes at the cost of unfinished work. There was no VPN back then, no remote access. I often slipped into the office at 3:00 AM, worked for a few hours, went home to nap, and then returned by 7:00 AM as if nothing had happened. No one knew the lengths I went to keep everything together: my job, my family, and my promise to a little boy.

As he grew, Bisrat naturally called me Dadi. I never corrected him. In his eyes, I was both uncle and father, and I wore that dual role with quiet pride.

Years later, when my brother came to visit, we decided it was time to set the record straight. We sat at the table, placed a photo of his father in front of him, and explained. "This is your father," we told him. He looked at me, confused. I nodded gently to assure him it was true.

We pointed to Tadesse. "This is your uncle."

He nodded again.

Then came the test. "And who is this?" they asked, pointing at me.

Bisrat looked at me, searching my eyes for confirmation. At last, he smiled and said with certainty: "That's my uncle Dadi."

The room erupted with laughter and tears at once. It was the most profound compliment I had ever received to be recognized not only as an uncle but also as the father figure who had walked beside him. Even now, as a grown professional, he still calls me Pops.

Reflection

Family is not defined by titles alone. Sometimes it is shaped by sacrifice, by presence, by the choice to step into a role that life leaves vacant. I was never just an uncle, and for me, he was never just a nephew.

Being "Uncle Dadi" taught me that love makes its own definitions. It was one of the earliest reminders in America that the bonds we build are as powerful and sometimes even stronger than those written in blood.

The Fall of the Pole

The fall of the pole left me with twisted hands, bones broken, chest ruptured, and arm in a cast. The doctor gave me ninety days to recover. I came back to work in ten days. I refused the worker's compensation check, writing on the back, "This body is not for sale." That fall marked me, but it did not stop me. It became a symbol: no matter how far I fell, I would rise again.

The 2011 Career Fall

Years later, I fell again, this time not from a pole, but from the height of my career. In 2011, without explanation, I was let go. The pain was just as sharp, but invisible. And just as before, I rose again, this time to become Division Vice President overseeing work across fifteen states. The body can heal bones. The spirit, if unbroken, can heal careers.

Fire and Light

In 1992, I returned to Ethiopia for the first time. I remembered the dim room where my mother and I had once spoken before I burned the letter of clemency, firelight fueled by fear and survival. Now, I returned with a wife and a child, carrying not flames of desperation but a modern television that lit her house. My mother became the first in her town to have a TV. The light of survival had been replaced by the glow of love and progress.

The Cheetah's Resolve

In Maryland, when a manager told me I would leave soon, like so many before me, I answered: "I am the Cheetah swift, calculating, and I won't let go until the work is done." That image stayed with me, for it summed up how I survived every trial. I was not the strongest, not the largest, but I was the most determined.

Enana - The Steady Flame

Through every rise and every fall, one constant anchored me: Enana. From the day we met, she stood beside me through every challenge, raising our children, managing the long nights when I was away, and enduring the disruption of moves across the country, each time building a home only to take everything down and start again in a place unknown.

When I traveled far and often, she bore the quiet weight of my absence. She shoveled snow alone while I sat in warm offices. She carried the burden of solitude while I carried the burden of responsibility. When I came home with my arm in a cast and my body bruised, she did not cast doubt or blame me for carelessness. She simply stood beside me, steady and unwavering.

My career, my family, my health, and even my resilience would not have been the same without her. Enana was not just a companion. She was the steady flame that kept the cold at bay, the strength that made my strength possible. If my story is one of resilience, hers is one of quiet courage and unshakable love.

Legacy for My Children

To Mahlet, Markos, and Bisrat: the lessons of my life are yours to inherit. I crossed deserts, fled war, endured prisons, and started with ten dollars in my pocket. I stumbled, fell, and rose again. What I want you to remember is not the hardship itself, but the truth behind it: that resilience, faith, and community can turn even the darkest path into light.

I leave you not riches, but stories. Not titles, but lessons. Not perfection, but proof that survival can grow into strength, and strength into legacy.

Epilogue

This book began as a way to preserve memories, but it has grown into something larger, a bridge between past and future. The steps I took across valleys, rivers, and foreign lands were not just my own. They carried the weight of generations before me and laid the ground for those yet to come.

In sharing my story, I hope I have also honored the resilience of those who walked beside me as family, friends, mentors, and communities that gave me strength when I was weak, and laughter when I was weary.

If there is one truth I have learned, it is that courage is not the absence of fear but the willingness to cross horizons despite it. As Max Ehrmann wrote in Desiderata:

"Beyond a wholesome discipline, be gentle with yourself. You are a child of the universe no less than the trees and the stars; you have a right to be here."

These words carried me when I felt out of place, a stranger in new lands, and they remain a reminder that every struggle has purpose.

I leave this story not as an ending, but as a beginning. May it inspire my children, my grandchildren, and anyone who reads it to know that even from the humblest start, even with obstacles as high as mountains, one can still rise, endure, and carve out a life of meaning.

With gratitude,

Zinah Mineyahl

Closing Quote

"A man who has crossed many rivers does not fear the rain." Ethiopian *Proverb*

Glossary of Ethiopian Terms

This glossary provides explanations of Ethiopian words, cultural references, and place names that appear throughout the memoir. It is designed to give readers especially those less familiar with Ethiopian history and traditions Kuyick and clear reference points without interrupting the flow of the story.

Glossary of Ethiopian Terms

Abaselma (አባስልማ)

A village in the Amhara region of Ethiopia.

Addis Ababa (አዲስ አበባ)

The capital city of Ethiopia, meaning 'New Flower'. It is the political, cultural, and economic center of the country.

Andabet (አንዳቤት)

A town in the Amhara region of Ethiopia.

Ato (አቶ) The Ethiopian equivalent to Mr.

Ayawa (አያዋ)

A traditional term of endearment or respect for men, often used with a name, e.g., 'Ayawa Fenta.'

Ayaya (አያያ)

A traditional term of endearment or respect for older men, similar to 'uncle.'

Brian Tracy - A Canadian American motivational speaker and author known for self-development books such as Eat That Frog! and Goals! His work emphasizes discipline, productivity, and the power of written goals.

Debre Markos (ደብረ ማርቆስ)

A city in the Amhara region of Ethiopia, significant as a cultural and historical center.

Dejazmach (ደጃዝማች)

Short for Dejenazmach, meaning Commander of the field a military title meaning commander of the central body of a traditional Ethiopian army formation composed of a forward or vanguard, the main central body, left and right flanks and a rearguard

Dejen (ደጆን)

A town in Gojjam, Ethiopia, often remembered as a crossing point on the way to Addis Ababa.

Derg (ደርግ)

The military junta that ruled Ethiopia from 1974 to 1991.

Desiderata

A 1927 prose poem by Max Ehrmann, widely quoted for its timeless advice on balance, humility, and resilience. Key lines guided the author during difficult moments, reminding him of his worth and the value of his journey.

Doqma (ዶቅማ)

A water berry is an evergreen tree of the genus Syzygium, commonly Syzygium cordatum, which grows in African forests and swampy areas. It produces edible, often red to dark-purple, fleshy fruit known as water berries, which are consumed by humans and various wildlife.

EDU

Ethiopian Democratic Union, a political movement formed in exile opposing the Derg regime. The EDU was in favor of the Haile Selassie regime.

ELF

Eritrean Liberation Front, one of the groups fighting for Eritrean independence from Ethiopia.

Entoto (እንጦጦ)

A mountain north of Addis Ababa with historical significance as the site of Menelik II's capital before Addis Ababa.

EPLF

Eritrean People's Liberation Front, the leading armed group in the Eritrean independence struggle.

EPRP

Ethiopian People's Revolutionary Party, a Marxist opposition party against the Derg regime.

Filwuha (ፍልዉሃ)

A natural hot spring in Addis Ababa, historically important for settlement and leisure.

Gashe (ጋሽ)

A respectful title for an elder man, similar to 'sir' or 'uncle.'

Gebsit (ገብሲት)

A small town in central Ethiopia in the Amhara region (Gojjam), the ancestral land of the author.

Grazmach (ግራዝማች)

A traditional Ethiopian military title meaning 'commander of the left.'

Gubaya (ጉባያ)

A village in Ethiopia, located in the Amhara region.

Humera (ሑመራ)

A town in northwestern Ethiopia, known for its agriculture and trade, located near the borders with Sudan and Eritrea.

Ietete (እቴቴ)

A term of respect or endearment for older women, similar to 'auntie.'

Imeye (እሜዮ)

A term we used to refer to our mother which is equivalent to mommy in the USA.

Italem (እታለም)

A traditional endearment for women, like 'dear lady.'

Itye (እትዬ)

A traditional endearment for women like Itete. The equivalent meaning when translated is my dear sister.

Kebele (ቀበሌ)

The smallest administrative unit in Ethiopia, similar to a neighborhood association or ward.

Kelabit (ቀላቢት)

A person who sells meals on a monthly contract.

Les Brown

An American motivational speaker, author, and former politician. Famous for his "You've got to be hungry!" philosophy, he inspires people to overcome fear, self-doubt, and setbacks to achieve greatness.

Medeb (መደብ)

A platform made of rock or wood, formed with mud and sealed with cow manure, used for various purposes.

Mene Dibayu (መነ ዲባዩ) –

Descendants of Ato Dibayu Legas. Author's grandfather was grandson of Ato Dibayu.

Selelkula (ሰለልኩላ)

A village in the Amhara region of Ethiopia.

Shema (ሸማ)

Traditional handwoven Ethiopian cloth, often used for clothing such as shawls and gabi.

Shiro (ሽሮ)

A staple Ethiopian dish made from powdered chickpeas or beans, often served as a stew.

Shitaye (ሽታየ) A household term of endearment we used to refer to our father.

Tela (ጠላ)

A traditional Ethiopian homemade beer brewed from barley, maize, or other grains.

TPLF

Tigray People's Liberation Front, a political and military organization in Ethiopia.

Tkurir (ትኩሪር)

Men from Sudan or Chad who lived in Humera and engaged in contraband trade.

Woyzero (ወይዘሮ)

The Ethiopian equivalent to Mrs.

Yetmen (የትመን)

A town in the Amhara region of Ethiopia.

Zeng (ዘንግ)

A long stick resembling the handle of a spear but without the spearhead.

Znar (ⵣⵏⴰⵔ)

A traditional handmade leather ammunition belt worn around the waist.

About the Author

Zinah Mineyahl's journey began in Debre Markos, Ethiopia. As a teenager, he fled political upheaval, spending years as a refugee before arriving in the United States in his early twenties. He carried with him only $10, broken English, and an unshakable determination to survive.

Starting at the bottom of the telecommunications industry, Zinah worked as a frontline cable installer, braving heat, attics, and long hours. His resilience and commitment to learning propelled him upward. Over the next 39 years, he advanced step by step into leadership, supervisor, manager, director, and ultimately Division Vice President of Workforce Operations.

Education was a cornerstone of his success. Along the way, in addition to his two-year degree in Digital Electronics, and a Bachelor of Science in Management he earned an MBA from SNHU with a specialization in consulting, pursued executive development at UCLA and Harvard, and continued to learn even after retirement. His professional achievements were matched by his passion for service: he served on three different non-profit organizations dedicating his time to the causes he believed in.

Yet for all his titles and accomplishments, Zinah's greatest pride has been his family. With his wife, Enana, he raised two children, Mahlet and Markos, through years of relocation and sacrifice. A proud U.S. citizen, he credits his success not only to his own determination but also to the support of mentors, friends, and above all, his family.

His memoir, The Courage to Cross Horizons, is both a testament to resilience and a gift to future generations: a reminder that even the harshest beginnings can lead to lives of purpose, dignity, and hope.